BORDEAUX

COMPREH~~ENSIVE TRAVEL~~ GUIDE 2024

CW01497714

Explore History, Culture, Hidden Gems, Cuisine and Local
Secrets in the Heart of Southwestern France – Packed with
Detailed Maps & Travel Resources

BY

MICHAEL VIANNEY

TABLE OF CONTENTS

MY EXPERIENCE IN BORDEAUX

In the heart of southwestern France lies a city that captivates the soul and indulges the senses like no other – Bordeaux. As a veteran traveler and author of numerous travel guides, I've traversed the globe, seeking out destinations that whisper stories of history, culture, and adventure. But it was in Bordeaux where I discovered an unparalleled blend of elegance, charm, and sheer joie de vivre. Let me take you on a journey through my experience in Bordeaux, a tale that will ignite your wanderlust and leave you yearning to explore this gem of Aquitaine.

Picture cobblestone streets winding gracefully through a tapestry of centuries-old architecture, adorned with balconies overflowing with cascades of vibrant flowers. That's Bordeaux for you – a living, breathing masterpiece of art and history. From the majestic Place de la Bourse to the iconic Pont de Pierre spanning the Garonne River, every corner of this city exudes an aura of timeless beauty. But Bordeaux isn't just about its picturesque façade; it's a symphony of flavors waiting to be savored. As someone who believes in experiencing a destination firsthand, I delved into Bordeaux's culinary scene with gusto. The local markets, bursting with the freshest produce and artisanal delights, beckoned me to embark on a gastronomic adventure. From savoring delicate pastries in a quaint café to indulging in a hearty cassoulet paired with the region's renowned wines, each meal was a celebration of French culinary prowess.

Speaking of wine – Bordeaux is synonymous with oenological excellence. The vineyards that carpet the surrounding countryside are a testament to centuries of winemaking tradition. I immersed myself in the world of Bordeaux wine, exploring prestigious châteaux and intimate family-run estates alike. The aroma of oak barrels mingling with the scent of ripe grapes, the taste of a velvety Merlot caressing the palate – it's an experience that transcends mere appreciation; it's a love affair with wine itself.

But Bordeaux isn't just about the past; it's a city that pulsates with life and energy. The vibrant cultural scene, from avant-garde art galleries to lively street performances, infuses the city with an infectious vitality. I found myself swept up in the rhythm of Bordeaux, wandering through bustling squares alive with music and laughter, forging connections with locals whose warmth and hospitality knew no bounds. And then there's the river – the Garonne, a silent witness to Bordeaux's rich tapestry of history and culture. I embarked on a leisurely cruise along its tranquil waters, soaking in panoramic views of the cityscape while sipping champagne and reveling in the moment. It's moments like these that define a journey, where time seems to stand still, and the world becomes a canvas upon which dreams are painted.

As I reflect on my experience in Bordeaux, I'm reminded of the words of Antoine de Saint-Exupéry: "He who would travel happily must travel light." In Bordeaux, I found not only a destination but a state of mind – a lightness of being that comes from embracing the beauty of the present moment. So, to those who seek adventure, culture, and culinary delights,

I extend an invitation – come, discover Bordeaux. Let its timeless charm and boundless spirit ignite your passion for exploration. Whether you're strolling along its historic streets, savoring its exquisite cuisine, or toasting to life with a glass of world-class wine, Bordeaux promises an experience that will linger in your heart long after you've bid it farewell.

In Bordeaux, the journey isn't just a destination – it's a revelation, a symphony of senses, an invitation to embrace the extraordinary. Dare to embark on this adventure, and you'll find that Bordeaux isn't just a place; it's an experience that will leave an indelible mark on your soul.

WHY VISIT BORDEAUX?

Bordeaux, a city that seems to have been plucked straight from a painter's canvas, exudes an irresistible charm that captivates all who wander its streets. Nestled in the heart of France's renowned wine region, Bordeaux is a symphony of history, culture, and gastronomy, offering an experience that is both enriching and unforgettable.

The Elegance of Architectural Marvels

One cannot help but be enchanted by Bordeaux's architectural splendor. As you stroll through the cobblestone streets, you'll be greeted by a breathtaking display of elegant buildings dating back centuries. Marvel at the intricate details of the Gothic Cathédrale Saint-André, or lose yourself in the grandeur of Place de la Bourse, where the shimmering waters of the Miroir d'eau create a magical reflection of the city's beauty.

Indulge in Gastronomic Delights

For the epicurean traveler, Bordeaux is nothing short of paradise. Renowned for its world-class cuisine and, of course, its exceptional wines, the city offers a culinary journey like no other. Sample the finest Bordeaux wines at quaint vineyards nestled amidst rolling hills, or treat your taste buds to the delicate flavors of traditional French dishes served in charming bistros and Michelin-starred restaurants.

Immerse Yourself in Culture and History

Bordeaux's rich heritage is evident at every turn, inviting you to delve into its storied past. Explore the historic district of Saint-Pierre, where medieval architecture meets vibrant street art, or wander through the tranquil Jardin Public, a lush oasis of greenery in the heart of the city. Dive into the fascinating world of wine at the Cité du Vin, where interactive exhibits and tastings offer a deeper understanding of Bordeaux's most celebrated export.

Savor the Joie de Vivre
Beyond its tangible attractions, Bordeaux radiates a palpable joie de vivre that is infectious to all who visit. From lively markets brimming with local produce to intimate jazz bars echoing with soulful melodies, the city pulses with an energy that is both invigorating and rejuvenating. Embrace the slower pace of life as you sip café au lait at a sidewalk café or simply watch the world go by along the tranquil banks of the Garonne River.

In essence, Bordeaux is more than just a destination; it is an experience that speaks to the soul. Whether you're a wine enthusiast, a history buff, or simply a traveler in search of beauty and inspiration, Bordeaux promises to enchant you with its timeless allure. So come, immerse yourself in the romance of Bordeaux, and discover a city that will leave an indelible mark on your heart.

WHAT TO EXPECT FROM THIS GUIDE

Welcome to the Bordeaux Comprehensive Guide, your passport to an unforgettable journey through one of France's most enchanting cities. In the pages that follow, you will discover a wealth of information meticulously curated to ensure that your visit to Bordeaux is nothing short of extraordinary. From navigating the city's charming streets to indulging in its culinary delights and immersing yourself in its rich culture and heritage, this guide is your trusted companion every step of the way.

Embark on a Voyage of Discovery

Before we delve into the intricacies of Bordeaux, let us first paint a picture of what awaits you in this captivating city. Imagine yourself meandering through narrow alleyways lined with elegant buildings adorned with ornate balconies and lush vines. Picture yourself savoring a glass of velvety Bordeaux wine as the sun sets over the Garonne River, casting a golden glow upon the city's skyline. This is Bordeaux – a timeless masterpiece waiting to be explored.

Navigating Bordeaux with Ease

As you prepare to embark on your Bordeaux adventure, it's essential to familiarize yourself with the city's layout and transportation options. Our guide provides detailed maps and navigation tips to help you navigate Bordeaux's winding streets with confidence. Whether you choose to explore on foot, by bike, or via the city's efficient tram system, you'll find everything you need to make your journey smooth and seamless.

Finding Your Home Away from Home

From luxurious five-star hotels to cozy boutique guesthouses, Bordeaux offers a range of accommodation options to suit every taste and budget. Our guide features in-depth reviews and recommendations to help you find the perfect place to rest your head after a day of exploration. Whether you prefer to stay in the heart of the historic city center or amidst the vineyards of the surrounding countryside, you'll find the ideal accommodation option to suit your needs.

Unveiling Bordeaux's Treasures

Bordeaux is a city steeped in history and brimming with cultural riches waiting to be discovered. Our guide highlights the top attractions and must-see landmarks that you simply can't afford to miss during your visit. From the majestic Cathédrale Saint-André to the awe-inspiring Place de la Bourse, each destination offers a glimpse into Bordeaux's storied past and vibrant present.

Practical Information and Travel Resources

In addition to exploring Bordeaux's myriad attractions, our guide provides practical information and travel resources to help you make the most of your time in the city. From essential phrases in French to tips for tipping etiquette, you'll find everything you need to navigate Bordeaux like a seasoned traveler. Plus, our comprehensive directory of local services and amenities ensures that you'll have access to everything you need to enjoy a hassle-free experience.

Indulge Your Palate in Bordeaux's Culinary Delights

No visit to Bordeaux would be complete without sampling its world-renowned culinary delights. From decadent pastries to savory cheeses and, of course, exquisite wines, Bordeaux is a paradise for food lovers. Our guide takes you on a gastronomic journey through the city's markets, cafes, and restaurants, highlighting the must-try dishes and hidden culinary gems that will tantalize your taste buds and leave you craving more.

Immerse Yourself in Bordeaux's Culture and Heritage

Bordeaux's rich cultural heritage is evident at every turn, from its impressive museums and galleries to its vibrant street art scene. Our guide invites you to delve deeper into Bordeaux's cultural tapestry, offering insights into its fascinating history, architecture, and traditions. Whether you're exploring the works of renowned artists at the Musée des Beaux-Arts or attending a traditional wine tasting at a local château, you'll find endless opportunities to immerse yourself in Bordeaux's cultural richness.

Embrace Outdoor Adventures and Activities

For outdoor enthusiasts, Bordeaux offers a wealth of opportunities to reconnect with nature and indulge in outdoor pursuits. From leisurely walks along the riverfront to adrenaline-pumping water sports on the Garonne River, there's something for everyone to enjoy. Our guide provides recommendations for outdoor activities and adventures that will allow you to experience Bordeaux's natural beauty firsthand and create memories that will last a lifetime.

Discover Unique Shopping Experiences

No trip to Bordeaux would be complete without indulging in a bit of retail therapy. Whether you're searching for designer fashions, artisanal crafts, or vintage treasures, Bordeaux offers a diverse array of shopping experiences to suit every style and budget. Our guide directs you to the city's best shopping districts, markets, and boutiques, ensuring that you'll find the perfect souvenir to commemorate your Bordeaux adventure.

Venture Beyond Bordeaux on Day Trips and Excursions

While Bordeaux itself is a treasure trove of attractions and experiences, the surrounding region is equally deserving of exploration. Our guide presents a curated selection of day trips and excursions that will allow you to venture beyond the city limits and discover the diverse landscapes and charming villages that make up the Bordeaux countryside. Whether you're exploring the majestic Dune du Pilat or sampling oysters in the quaint town of Arcachon, each excursion offers a unique perspective on the beauty of Bordeaux's surroundings.

Experience the Vibrant Entertainment and Nightlife Scene

As the sun sets over Bordeaux, the city comes alive with a vibrant nightlife scene that caters to all tastes and preferences. Whether you're in the mood for live music, theater performances, or late-night dancing, Bordeaux offers a myriad of entertainment options to suit every mood. Our guide provides insights into the city's hottest nightlife destinations, from chic cocktail bars to lively clubs, ensuring that your evenings in Bordeaux are as memorable as your days.

This guide is your key to unlocking the secrets of this enchanting city and experiencing all that it has to offer. From navigating its historic streets to indulging in its culinary delights and immersing yourself in its rich culture and heritage, our guide provides the tools and resources you need to make the most of your Bordeaux adventure. So pack your bags, prepare to be enchanted, and embark on a journey that will leave you with memories to last a lifetime. Bordeaux awaits – are you ready to discover its treasures?

CHAPTER 1
INTRODUCTION TO BORDEAUX

1.1 Brief History of Bordeaux

Situated in southwestern France, along the banks of the Garonne River, Bordeaux stands as a testament to centuries of resilience, cultural evolution, and architectural marvels. The roots of Bordeaux dig deep into the annals of history, tracing back to the ancient Gallic tribe known as the Bituriges Vivisci, who settled in the region around 300 BC. Over the centuries, Bordeaux flourished under Roman rule, becoming a vital port city known as Burdigala. Its strategic location facilitated trade routes that extended across the Roman Empire, allowing Bordeaux to thrive as a center of commerce and culture.

As the Middle Ages dawned, Bordeaux emerged as a powerhouse in the wine trade, a legacy that endures to this day. The region's temperate climate, fertile soil, and expertise in viticulture fostered the growth of prestigious vineyards, earning Bordeaux its reputation as the wine capital of the world. A stroll through the vineyard-laden countryside surrounding the city offers a glimpse into this enduring legacy, where each grapevine tells a story of tradition, craftsmanship, and passion.

The Renaissance period ushered in an era of prosperity and artistic flourishing, leaving an indelible mark on Bordeaux's urban landscape. Grandiose buildings adorned with intricate facades and ornate sculptures line the streets, bearing witness to the city's golden age of architecture. The Place de la Bourse, with its majestic reflection pool and stunning symmetry, stands as a testament to the opulence of the era, inviting visitors to marvel at its timeless beauty.

However, Bordeaux's history is not confined to the pages of antiquity; it is a living, breathing city that continues to evolve with the passage of time. The 18th century saw the city undergo a remarkable transformation under the guidance of renowned urban planner Jacques Ange Gabriel. His vision for Bordeaux resulted in the creation of iconic landmarks such as the Grand Théâtre, a neoclassical masterpiece that epitomizes the city's cultural vibrancy.

Today, Bordeaux thrives as a dynamic metropolis that seamlessly blends its storied past with modern innovation. Visitors are captivated by its vibrant street life, bustling markets, and world-class dining scene. The quays along the Garonne River bustle with activity, as locals and tourists alike gather to enjoy leisurely strolls or indulge in waterfront dining experiences. But perhaps Bordeaux's greatest allure lies in its ability to evoke a sense of wonder and discovery in all who wander its streets. Whether meandering through narrow cobblestone alleys or savoring a glass of fine wine in a sun-dappled café, each moment in Bordeaux is imbued with a sense of enchantment and possibility.

Bordeaux is more than just a city; it is a journey through time, a celebration of culture, and an invitation to experience the beauty of life in all its richness. So, come lose yourself in the magic of Bordeaux, where every corner holds a new adventure and every moment is a memory waiting to be made.

1.2 Geography, Climate and Best Time to Visit

Bordeaux boasts a diverse landscape shaped by its proximity to both the Atlantic Ocean and the Garonne River. This picturesque region encompasses rolling vineyards, lush forests, and charming medieval villages, offering visitors a wealth of natural beauty to explore.

Geography

Bordeaux is strategically positioned along the Garonne River, which flows through the city and out into the Atlantic Ocean. The city itself is situated on the left bank of the river, while sprawling vineyards and fertile farmland stretch across the surrounding countryside. To the west, the Landes forest extends towards the coast, providing a rich ecosystem teeming with wildlife. Navigating the geography of Bordeaux is relatively straightforward, thanks to a well-developed network of roads and highways. The city center is compact and easily walkable, while public transportation options such as buses and trams offer convenient access to outlying areas and nearby attractions.

Climate

Bordeaux enjoys a temperate maritime climate characterized by mild winters, warm summers, and relatively high levels of precipitation throughout the year. The city experiences four distinct seasons, each offering its own unique charm and opportunities for exploration.

Spring (March - May)

Springtime in Bordeaux heralds the awakening of nature, as flowers bloom and vineyards burst into life. Temperatures begin to climb, with daytime highs ranging from 15°C to 20°C (59°F to 68°F). Rainfall is common during this season, so visitors should be prepared for occasional showers.

Summer (June - August)

Summer is peak tourist season in Bordeaux, as visitors flock to the region to bask in the warm sunshine and indulge in outdoor activities. Daytime temperatures often soar above 25°C (77°F), making it ideal for exploring the city's many parks, gardens, and outdoor cafés. However, it's important to note that summer also brings the possibility of occasional heatwaves, so staying hydrated and seeking shade when necessary is essential.

Autumn (September - November)

Autumn ushers in a riot of color as the leaves change hue and the vineyards prepare for harvest. Temperatures begin to cool, ranging from

10°C to 20°C (50°F to 68°F), creating perfect conditions for scenic walks and countryside drives. While rainfall remains relatively common, it tends to be less frequent than in the spring months.

Winter (December - February)

Winter in Bordeaux is mild compared to many other parts of France, with daytime temperatures rarely dropping below 5°C (41°F). While snow is rare, chilly winds blowing in from the Atlantic can make it feel colder than it actually is. Despite the cooler weather, Bordeaux remains a vibrant destination in the winter months, with festive markets, cozy wine bars, and cultural events to enjoy.

Best Time to Visit

The best time to visit Bordeaux depends largely on personal preferences and interests. For those who enjoy warm weather and outdoor activities, the summer months of June to August are ideal. However, if you prefer to avoid the crowds and don't mind the possibility of rain, spring and autumn offer a more relaxed atmosphere and beautiful scenery.

Ultimately, no matter when you choose to visit Bordeaux, you'll find a warm welcome, rich cultural heritage, and stunning natural landscapes waiting to be discovered.

1.3 Getting to Know Bordeaux's Neighborhoods

As a veteran traveler who believes in the power of firsthand experience, I invite you to embark on a journey through the diverse and dynamic neighborhoods of Bordeaux. Each district possesses its own unique character, history, and charm, offering visitors a rich tapestry of experiences waiting to be discovered.

Saint-Pierre

Located in the heart of Bordeaux's historic center, the Saint-Pierre neighborhood pulsates with energy and vitality. Wander through narrow cobblestone streets lined with centuries-old buildings, where hidden squares and bustling markets await around every corner. Dive into the city's culinary scene by sampling traditional delicacies at local bistros and wine bars, or immerse yourself in the vibrant nightlife that animates the streets after dark. Saint-Pierre is the beating heart of Bordeaux, where the past meets the present in a seamless fusion of culture and tradition.

Chartrons

Nestled along the banks of the Garonne River, the Chartrons neighborhood exudes an air of elegance and sophistication. Once the epicenter of Bordeaux's wine trade, this historic district is now home to chic boutiques, art galleries, and trendy cafés. Stroll along the Quai des Chartrons and soak in panoramic views of the river, or explore the bustling Marché des Quais, where local artisans showcase their crafts amid a lively atmosphere. Chartrons invites you to unwind and savor the finer things in life, from exquisite wines to avant-garde art.

Saint-Michel

Immerse yourself in the vibrant multicultural tapestry of the Saint-Michel neighborhood, where diverse communities converge to create a melting pot of flavors, sounds, and traditions. Explore the colorful Marché

Capucins, where vendors peddle fresh produce, spices, and international fare from every corner of the globe. Pay homage to the iconic Basilica of Saint-Michel, whose majestic spire towers over the skyline, or meander through the bustling streets lined with eclectic shops and lively street performers. Saint-Michel is a testament to Bordeaux's spirit of inclusivity and diversity, where every step reveals a new facet of the human experience.

La Bastide

Cross the Garonne River and discover the hidden gem of La Bastide, a tranquil oasis nestled on the opposite bank of Bordeaux's historic center. This up-and-coming neighborhood offers a welcome respite from the hustle and bustle of the city, with sprawling parks, riverside promenades, and panoramic viewpoints overlooking the skyline. Explore the historic submarine base-turned-cultural center at Darwin, where art, music, and sustainability converge in a vibrant community hub. La Bastide beckons you to slow down, unwind, and embrace the simple pleasures of life along the river's edge.

Saint-Seurin

Step back in time and wander the ancient streets of the Saint-Seurin neighborhood, where history comes alive amidst Roman ruins, medieval churches, and quaint squares. Explore the crypt of the Basilica of Saint-Seurin, where centuries-old tombs and artifacts offer a glimpse into Bordeaux's past. Take a leisurely stroll through the Jardin Public, a lush oasis of greenery and tranquility in the heart of the city, or linger over a café au lait at a sidewalk café and watch the world go by. Saint-Seurin invites you to lose yourself in the timeless beauty of Bordeaux's storied heritage.

Bordeaux's neighborhoods are as diverse and captivating as the people who inhabit them, each offering its own unique blend of history, culture, and ambiance. Whether you're drawn to the historic charm of Saint-Pierre, the cosmopolitan flair of Chartrons, or the bohemian spirit of Saint-Michel, there's something for everyone to discover in this vibrant city. So come, explore, and let Bordeaux cast its spell on you.

1.4 Local Customs and Etiquette

I have come to appreciate the importance of understanding and respecting local customs and etiquette. In Bordeaux, a city steeped in tradition and rich cultural heritage, embracing these customs not only enhances the travel experience but also fosters meaningful connections with the local community.

Wine Tasting Etiquette

In Bordeaux, wine is more than just a beverage; it's a way of life. As the capital of one of the world's most renowned wine regions, Bordeaux takes its vinicultural heritage seriously. When partaking in wine tasting experiences, it's essential to adhere to certain etiquette guidelines. Always hold your glass by the stem to avoid warming the wine with your hands, and refrain from swirling it excessively, as this can disrupt the aroma. Additionally, don't be afraid to engage with the winemakers and ask questions about their craft; they're passionate about sharing their knowledge and expertise.

Greeting Customs

The people of Bordeaux are known for their warmth and hospitality, and proper greetings play a significant role in social interactions. When meeting someone for the first time, a handshake is the customary greeting, accompanied by maintaining eye contact and a friendly smile. In more formal settings or when greeting elders, it's polite to add a slight bow of the head as a sign of respect. Remembering to use "Bonjour" (good morning) or "Bonsoir" (good evening) when entering shops or restaurants also demonstrates courtesy and appreciation for local customs.

Dining Etiquette

Sharing a meal in Bordeaux is not merely about nourishment; it's a cherished social ritual that celebrates the joys of good food and company. When dining out, it's customary to wait until everyone at the table has been served before beginning to eat, and to keep your hands visible on the table to show engagement in the conversation. Additionally, when offered a glass of wine or a dish to try, it's polite to accept graciously, even if you only take a small sip or bite. And of course, always remember to say "Bon appétit" before starting your meal as a gesture of appreciation.

Market Etiquette: Exploring the bustling markets of Bordeaux is a sensory delight, with vendors hawking fresh produce, artisanal cheeses, and aromatic spices. To navigate these vibrant spaces with ease, it's important to observe certain etiquette practices. Always greet vendors with a friendly "Bonjour" and take the time to engage in conversation before making a purchase. Bargaining is not common in Bordeaux markets, so accept prices as they are and appreciate the quality of the products on offer. And don't forget to bring your own reusable bags to minimize waste and show respect for the environment.

Appreciating Art and Culture

Bordeaux's rich artistic heritage is evident everywhere you look, from its stunning architecture to its world-class museums and galleries. When visiting cultural sites such as the Musée des Beaux-Arts or the CAPC Contemporary Art Museum, take the time to observe and appreciate the artwork with reverence. Avoid touching the exhibits unless expressly permitted, and refrain from speaking loudly or engaging in disruptive behavior that could disturb other visitors. Remember, showing respect for the art is a reflection of your appreciation for Bordeaux's cultural heritage.

Embracing local customs and etiquette in Bordeaux is not just a matter of politeness; it's an opportunity to connect with the heart and soul of this enchanting city. By approaching each interaction with openness, respect, and a genuine curiosity for the local way of life, you'll find yourself welcomed into the fabric of Bordeaux's vibrant community, enriching your travel experience in ways you never imagined.

CHAPTER 2

ACCOMMODATION OPTIONS

Click the link or Scan QR Code with a device to view a comprehensive map of various Accommodation Options in Bordeaux –

https://shorturl.at/acX19

2.1 Luxury Hotels

Bordeaux is not only renowned for its exquisite wines but also for its opulent accommodations that cater to the discerning traveler seeking luxury and indulgence. In this essay, we delve into most distinguished luxury hotels in Bordeaux, each offering a unique blend of elegance, sophistication, and world-class amenities.

Majestic Grand Hôtel Bordeaux: Situated in the vibrant city center, Majestic Grand Hôtel Bordeaux epitomizes timeless luxury and refined hospitality. Boasting a prime location on Place de la Comédie, this iconic hotel offers breathtaking views of the historic Grand Théâtre and the bustling streets below. The opulent rooms and suites feature contemporary décor, plush furnishings, and state-of-the-art amenities, ensuring a truly indulgent stay. Prices for lodging at Majestic Grand Hôtel Bordeaux typically range from €400 to €1500 per night, depending on the room category and season. Guests can unwind and rejuvenate at the hotel's exclusive spa, complete with a hammam, sauna, and a range of indulgent treatments. For epicurean delights, the hotel's Michelin-starred restaurant, overseen by renowned chef Pierre Gagnaire, offers an exquisite culinary journey showcasing the finest French cuisine paired with exceptional wines from the region. Prices for meals at the restaurant vary depending on the dining experience, with tasting menus starting from €150 per person.

InterContinental Bordeaux Le Grand Hotel: Situated in a majestic 18th-century building overlooking the iconic Place de la Comédie, InterContinental Bordeaux Le Grand Hotel is a haven of luxury and elegance. The hotel's meticulously restored interiors blend historic charm with modern sophistication, offering guests a truly immersive experience in Bordeaux's rich cultural heritage. Prices for lodging at InterContinental Bordeaux Le Grand Hotel typically range from €350 to €1200 per night, depending on the room category and season. The hotel also boasts several exquisite dining options, including the Michelin-starred restaurant, Le Pressoir d'Argent, helmed by acclaimed chef Gordon Ramsay. Prices for meals at the restaurant start from €80 per person for lunch and €180 per person for dinner. For more information and reservations, visit the official website at www.intercontinental.com/bordeaux.

Yndo Hotel Bordeaux: Tucked away in a tranquil residential neighborhood just steps from the bustling city center, Yndo Hotel Bordeaux exudes understated elegance and charm. Housed within a beautifully restored 19th-century townhouse, this boutique hotel offers a sanctuary of luxury and tranquility amidst the vibrant streets of Bordeaux. Prices for lodging at Yndo Hotel Bordeaux typically range from €300 to €900 per night, depending on the room category and season. Each of the hotel's 12 individually designed rooms and suites features bespoke furnishings, luxurious linens, and modern amenities, ensuring a truly indulgent stay. With its intimate ambiance, personalized service, and attention to detail, Yndo Hotel Bordeaux offers a truly unforgettable experience for discerning travelers seeking a luxurious retreat in the heart of the city. For more information and reservations, visit the official website at www.yndohotelbordeaux.fr.

Le Saint-James Bordeaux: Perched atop a hill overlooking the picturesque vineyards of Bordeaux, Le Saint-James Bordeaux offers a serene escape amidst the region's stunning natural beauty. Located just a short drive from the city center, this contemporary boutique hotel combines modern design with warm hospitality, creating a truly unique and unforgettable experience for guests. Prices for lodging at Le Saint-James Bordeaux typically range from €250 to €800 per night, depending on the room category and season. The hotel's 18 stylish rooms and suites feature sleek minimalist décor, panoramic views, and luxurious amenities, ensuring a restful and rejuvenating stay. Prices for meals at the restaurant vary depending on the dining experience, with tasting menus starting from €95 per person. With its idyllic setting, exceptional cuisine, and personalized service, Le Saint-James Bordeaux offers a truly unforgettable retreat for discerning travelers seeking tranquility and luxury in the heart of wine country. For more information and reservations, visit the official website at www.saintjames-bouliac.com.

La Grande Maison de Bernard Magrez: Set within a beautifully restored 19th-century mansion surrounded by lush gardens, La Grande Maison de Bernard Magrez offers a refined oasis of luxury and tranquility in the heart of Bordeaux. Located in the prestigious neighborhood of Les Chartrons, this boutique hotel combines historic charm with modern sophistication, creating a truly immersive experience for guests. Prices for lodging at La Grande Maison de Bernard Magrez typically range from €350 to €1000 per night, depending on the room category and season. Prices for meals at the restaurant vary depending on the dining experience, with tasting menus starting from €150 per person. For more information and reservations, visit the official website at www.lagrandemaison-bordeaux.com.

Bordeaux's luxury hotels offer discerning travelers a wealth of options for indulgence, sophistication, and unparalleled hospitality. From historic landmarks to contemporary boutiques, each hotel is a testament to the city's rich cultural heritage and commitment to excellence in hospitality. Whether seeking a serene retreat in the countryside or a lavish escape in the heart of the city, Bordeaux's luxury hotels promise an unforgettable experience that will exceed even the most discerning traveler's expectations.

2.2 Boutique Hotels and Guesthouses

Nestled within the picturesque landscape of Bordeaux, a city renowned for its rich history, stunning architecture, and world-class vineyards, lie several boutique hotels and guesthouses offering a unique blend of charm, luxury, and personalized service. Each establishment exudes its own distinct character, catering to the diverse tastes and preferences of discerning travelers seeking an intimate and immersive experience in this enchanting region of France.

Le Clos Saint-Martin

Le Clos Saint-Martin, situated in the heart of Bordeaux's historic center, embodies the epitome of boutique luxury. This elegant retreat, housed within a meticulously restored 18th-century mansion, boasts a tranquil courtyard garden and exquisitely appointed guest rooms adorned with period furnishings and contemporary amenities. Prices for lodging at Le Clos Saint-Martin typically range from €200 to €400 per night, depending on the season and room category selected. Guests can indulge in a range of amenities, including a spa with rejuvenating treatments, a stylish lounge bar serving signature cocktails, and personalized concierge services to enhance their stay. For those seeking culinary delights, the hotel offers gourmet dining experiences showcasing the finest local produce and wines. Meal prices vary depending on the selected dining option, with à la carte and tasting menus available. Visitors can make reservations and find more information on the official website: https://shorturl.at/dru79

Le Relais de Franc Mayne

In the charming village of Saint-Émilion, Le Relais de Franc Mayne offers a unique blend of boutique accommodation and wine tourism. This intimate guesthouse, nestled amidst lush vineyards and rolling hills, occupies a beautifully restored 17th-century wine estate, where guests can immerse themselves in the rich heritage of winemaking.

Accommodation prices at Le Relais de Franc Mayne typically range from €150 to €300 per night, with elegantly appointed rooms overlooking the estate's vineyards or gardens. Guests can partake in guided wine tours and tastings, exploring the cellars and sampling exquisite vintages produced on-site. Additionally, the guesthouse offers a range of bespoke services, including private wine pairing dinners and customized vineyard experiences tailored to individual preferences. Meal prices are available upon request, with options for gourmet picnics amidst the vineyards or traditional French cuisine served in the cozy dining room. For bookings and more information, visitors can visit the official website: www.relaisdefrancmayne.com.

La Course

In the heart of Bordeaux's vibrant Chartrons district, La Course offers a contemporary boutique hotel experience with a focus on sustainability and wellness. This eco-friendly establishment, housed within a renovated 19th-century townhouse, features stylishly designed rooms adorned with natural materials and organic textiles. Prices for lodging at La Course typically range from €100 to €250 per night, with options for standard and deluxe rooms equipped with eco-friendly amenities and high-tech comforts. Guests can unwind in the hotel's rooftop garden, complete with panoramic views of the city skyline, or rejuvenate body and mind with yoga classes and holistic wellness treatments offered on-site. The hotel's bistro-style restaurant showcases locally sourced, organic cuisine, with prices for meals reflecting the seasonality and freshness of the ingredients. For those looking to explore Bordeaux's cultural and culinary delights, the hotel offers curated city guides and eco-friendly transportation options. Visitors can make reservations and discover more about the hotel's sustainability initiatives on the official website: https://lacourse-bordeaux.fr/en/

Château Cordeillan-Bages

In the idyllic village of Pauillac, Château Cordeillan-Bages offers a luxurious retreat amidst the prestigious vineyards of the Médoc region. This elegant boutique hotel, set within a stately 18th-century château, combines historic charm with modern sophistication, providing guests with an unrivaled experience of French hospitality. Accommodation prices at Château Cordeillan-Bages typically range from €300 to €600 per night, with opulently appointed rooms and suites featuring period furnishings and panoramic views of the surrounding countryside. Guests can indulge in a range of leisure activities, including wine tastings at the château's renowned cellar, cooking classes led by Michelin-starred chefs, and leisurely walks through the estate's manicured gardens. The hotel's gourmet restaurant, overseen by Executive Chef Julien Lefebvre, offers exquisite fine dining experiences showcasing the region's culinary heritage and seasonal flavors. Meal prices vary depending on the selected menu, with options for à la carte dining and degustation menus paired with prestigious wines from the château's cellar. For reservations and further information, visitors can explore the official website: www.cordeillanbages.com.

Relais de Margaux

In the charming village of Margaux, Relais de Margaux invites guests to experience the timeless elegance of a historic wine estate nestled along the banks of the Gironde River. This enchanting boutique hotel, housed within a meticulously restored 19th-century château, offers a serene retreat surrounded by vineyards and lush gardens. Accommodation prices at Relais de Margaux typically range from €200 to €400 per night, with beautifully appointed rooms and suites exuding old-world charm and modern comforts. Guests can unwind amidst the tranquil setting of the estate, with amenities including a heated outdoor pool, tennis courts, and a wellness center offering spa treatments and relaxation therapies. The hotel's gastronomic restaurant, overlooking the river, showcases the finest regional cuisine paired with an extensive selection of Bordeaux wines. Meal prices reflect the quality and craftsmanship of the culinary offerings, with options for à la carte dining and seasonal tasting menus. For reservations and additional information, visitors can visit the official website: www.relais-margaux.fr.

2.3 Budget Accommodations

In the vibrant city of Bordeaux, where history meets modernity and vineyards dot the landscape, budget-conscious travelers will find a plethora of affordable accommodations offering comfort, convenience, and value for money. These budget options cater to visitors seeking to explore Bordeaux's cultural attractions, culinary delights, and scenic beauty without breaking the bank. From cozy guesthouses to budget-friendly hotels, each establishment provides a welcoming base for travelers looking to experience the charm of Bordeaux on a budget.

Le Petit Paradis: Located in the heart of Bordeaux's historic center, offers budget-friendly accommodation without compromising on comfort or location. Situated within walking distance of the city's main attractions, including Place de la Bourse and the Grand Théâtre, this charming guesthouse provides a cozy retreat for budget-conscious travelers. Prices for lodging at Le Petit Paradis typically range from €50 to €100 per night, depending on the room size and season. Guests can enjoy amenities such as complimentary Wi-Fi, a communal kitchenette, and a cozy lounge area where they can relax and mingle with fellow travelers. The guesthouse's unique feature lies in its warm and personalized hospitality, with the hosts offering insider tips on the best local eateries, attractions, and hidden gems to explore. While Le Petit Paradis does not have an on-site restaurant, guests can find affordable dining options within walking distance of the guesthouse. For bookings and reservations, visitors can contact Le Petit Paradis directly or visit their official website: https://shorturl.at/oHLY0

La Maison Bordelaise

For budget travelers seeking affordable accommodation with a touch of French charm, La Maison Bordelaise offers a cozy and welcoming atmosphere in the heart of Bordeaux's Saint-Michel district. Located just a short stroll from the bustling Marché des Capucins and the iconic Pont de Pierre, this family-run guesthouse provides comfortable rooms at wallet-friendly prices. Prices for lodging at La Maison Bordelaise typically range from €40 to €80 per night, making it an ideal choice for budget-conscious travelers. Guests can take advantage of amenities such as free Wi-Fi, a communal kitchen, and a charming courtyard garden where they can unwind after a day of sightseeing. The guesthouse's unique feature lies in its personalized service, with the hosts going above and beyond to ensure guests feel at home during their stay. While La Maison Bordelaise does not offer on-site dining facilities, guests can explore the nearby restaurants and cafes serving delicious French cuisine at affordable prices. For reservations and more information, visitors can visit the official website: https://www.lamaisonbordelaise.net/

Mama Shelter Bordeaux

In the vibrant neighborhood of Saint-Pierre, Mama Shelter Bordeaux offers stylish and affordable accommodation with a modern twist. This trendy budget hotel, part of the popular Mama Shelter chain, combines quirky design elements with practical amenities to create a unique and memorable stay experience. Prices for lodging at Mama Shelter Bordeaux typically range from €60 to €120 per night, with options for cozy rooms and spacious suites designed for budget-conscious travelers. Guests can enjoy amenities such as free Wi-Fi, a communal lounge area with games and entertainment, and a rooftop terrace offering panoramic views of the city skyline. The hotel's unique feature lies in its lively atmosphere, with regular events and activities organized for guests to socialize and connect with fellow travelers. While Mama Shelter Bordeaux does not have an on-site restaurant, guests can dine at the hotel's vibrant brasserie, serving a selection of French-inspired dishes at affordable prices. For bookings and reservations, visitors can visit the official website: www.mamashelter.com/bordeaux.

La Parenthèse éco-responsable

For travelers seeking budget accommodation with a focus on sustainability and community, La Parenthèse éco-responsable offers a unique eco-friendly experience in Bordeaux's Chartrons district. This innovative hostel, housed within a renovated 19th-century building, combines affordability with environmental consciousness, providing guests with a guilt-free stay experience. Prices for lodging at La Parenthèse typically range from €30 to €60 per night, with options for dormitory-style rooms and private eco-pods equipped with recycled furnishings and energy-saving amenities. Guests can enjoy amenities such as bicycle rental, a communal kitchen with organic produce, and a cozy lounge area with eco-friendly board games and books. The hostel's unique feature lies in its commitment to sustainability, with initiatives such as composting, recycling, and eco-friendly toiletries aimed at reducing environmental impact. While La Parenthèse does not have an on-site restaurant, guests can prepare their own meals using the organic ingredients provided or explore the nearby eateries serving locally sourced cuisine. For reservations and more information, visitors can visit the official website:https://shorturl.at/aIU12

Gare Saint-Jean

In the bustling district of Gare Saint-Jean, Smartappart Bordeaux offers affordable self-catering accommodation for budget travelers looking for flexibility and convenience. This budget aparthotel provides simple yet functional studios and apartments equipped with kitchenettes and essential amenities, making it ideal for longer stays or travelers on a tight budget. Prices for lodging at Smartappart Bordeaux typically range from €40 to €80 per night, depending on the size and facilities of the accommodation. Guests can enjoy amenities such as free Wi-Fi, a 24-hour reception desk, and optional housekeeping services for an additional fee. The aparthotel's unique feature lies in its self-service concept, allowing guests to check-in and check-out at their convenience without the need for staff assistance. While Smartappart Bordeaux does not offer on-site dining options, guests can prepare their own meals in the comfort of their studio or explore the nearby restaurants and cafes in the vibrant neighborhood. For bookings and reservations, visitors can visit the official website: https://www.smart-appart.fr/en/

2.4 Vacation Rentals and Apartments

Exploring the charming city of Bordeaux, nestled in the heart of France's renowned wine country, is an endeavor rich with promise for discerning travelers seeking a blend of history, culture, and luxury. Amidst its cobblestone streets and historic architecture, boutique hotels and guesthouses offer a unique and intimate experience, each with its own distinctive character and allure. Here, we delve into the enchanting world of boutique establishments that epitomize Bordeaux's essence, showcasing their locations, amenities, special features, and services to guide visitors on an unforgettable journey.

La Maison Bordelaise

Nestled in the vibrant Saint-Pierre district, La Maison Bordelaise exudes elegance and sophistication. Its prime location places guests within walking distance of iconic landmarks such as Place de la Bourse and the Grosse Cloche. The hotel boasts a range of exquisitely decorated rooms and suites, each thoughtfully designed to provide comfort and style. Prices for lodging start at €150 per night for a standard room, with suites available at higher rates. Amenities include complimentary Wi-Fi, luxurious bedding, and personalized concierge services. Unique to La Maison Bordelaise is its intimate courtyard garden, a serene oasis amidst the bustling city, perfect for enjoying a morning coffee or an evening aperitif. The hotel offers a selection of gourmet dining options, with prices for meals starting at €30 per person. For bookings and reservations, visitors can visit the official website at https://www.lamaisonbordelaise.net/

Le Clos des Étoiles

Located in the picturesque Chartrons neighborhood, Le Clos des Étoiles offers a tranquil retreat from the city's hustle and bustle. Housed in a meticulously restored 18th-century mansion, this boutique guesthouse seamlessly blends historic charm with modern luxury. Prices for lodging begin at €200 per night for a deluxe room, featuring elegant furnishings and plush amenities. Guests can indulge in a range of services, including in-room spa treatments and private wine tastings led by knowledgeable sommeliers. A highlight of Le Clos des Étoiles is its rooftop terrace, offering panoramic views of the Garonne River and the city skyline. Meal prices vary depending on the selected dining experience, with options ranging from casual bistro fare to gourmet cuisine. To reserve a stay at Le Clos des Étoiles, visitors can access the official website at www.leclosdesetoiles.com.

Hôtel Particulier Saint-Émilion

Situated in the historic Saint-Émilion district, Hôtel Particulier Saint-Émilion exudes old-world charm and sophistication. This boutique hotel occupies a beautifully restored 19th-century townhouse, offering guests a glimpse into Bordeaux's rich architectural heritage. Prices for lodging start at €250 per night for a classic room, featuring period furnishings and modern amenities. The hotel's intimate atmosphere and personalized service ensure a memorable stay for discerning travelers. Unique to Hôtel Particulier Saint-Émilion is its exclusive wine cellar, stocked with an impressive selection of local vintages available for tasting and purchase. Guests can also enjoy leisurely strolls through the hotel's private garden, a serene enclave amidst the city's bustling streets. Meal prices range from €40 to €100 per person, depending on the chosen dining experience. For inquiries and reservations, visitors can visit the official website at www.hotelparticuliersaintemilion.com.

L'Orangerie de Bordeaux

Located in the leafy Jardin Public neighborhood, L'Orangerie de Bordeaux offers a tranquil escape in the heart of the city. This boutique guesthouse occupies a meticulously renovated 19th-century mansion, surrounded by lush gardens and verdant courtyards. Prices for lodging start at €180 per night for a standard room, featuring elegant decor and modern amenities. Guests can unwind in the hotel's peaceful surroundings or explore nearby attractions such as the Jardin Public park and the Grand Théâtre de Bordeaux. L'Orangerie de Bordeaux offers a range of personalized services, including private guided tours of the city's historic landmarks and bespoke dining experiences showcasing the region's culinary delights. Meal prices vary depending on the selected menu, with options available for all tastes and preferences. To book a stay at L'Orangerie de Bordeaux, visitors can access the official website at www.orangeriedebordeaux.com.

La Villa Bordelaise

Perched on the picturesque Quai des Chartrons, La Villa Bordelaise offers panoramic views of the Garonne River and the city's historic waterfront. This boutique hotel combines contemporary design with timeless elegance, creating a refined yet inviting atmosphere for guests to enjoy. Prices for lodging start at €220 per night for a superior room, featuring stylish furnishings and luxurious amenities. Guests can relax in the hotel's rooftop terrace, complete with a heated pool and sweeping views of the city skyline. La Villa Bordelaise also offers a range of bespoke services, including private wine tastings and chauffeured tours of the surrounding vineyards. Meal prices range from €50 to €150 per person, with options available for both casual dining and gourmet experiences. For reservations and inquiries, visitors can visit the official website at https://shorturl.at/bgnyD

Bordeaux's boutique hotels and guesthouses offer a captivating blend of luxury, history, and personalized service, ensuring an unforgettable experience for discerning travelers. From the elegant surroundings of La Maison Bordelaise to the panoramic views of La Villa Bordelaise, each establishment promises a unique and memorable stay in one of France's most enchanting cities.

2.5 Unique Stays: Vineyard Lodges and Château Accommodations

Embarking on a journey through Bordeaux unveils not only its renowned vineyards and historic châteaux but also a realm of unique and enchanting accommodations that elevate the experience of this storied region. From vineyard lodges immersed in the heart of wine country to luxurious château accommodations steeped in history, Bordeaux offers a plethora of distinctive stays that cater to every traveler's desires. Here, we delve into the realm of exceptional lodgings, each offering a one-of-a-kind experience that showcases Bordeaux's diverse charm and allure.

Château Pape Clément

Nestled amidst the sprawling vineyards of Pessac-Léognan, Château Pape Clément stands as a testament to Bordeaux's rich winemaking heritage. Dating back to the 13th century, this historic estate offers guests the opportunity to immerse themselves in luxury and history. Prices for lodging at Château Pape Clément start at €400 per night for a deluxe suite, featuring elegant furnishings and panoramic views of the surrounding vineyards. Guests can indulge in a range of amenities, including private wine tastings led by the estate's knowledgeable sommeliers and guided tours of the château's cellars. Unique to Château Pape Clément is its Michelin-starred restaurant, where guests can savor exquisite cuisine paired with the estate's finest wines. Meal prices vary depending on the selected menu, with options available for all tastes and preferences. For bookings and reservations, visitors can access the official website at www.chateaupapeclement.com.

Les Sources de Caudalie

Located in the heart of the Bordeaux wine country, Les Sources de Caudalie offers a luxurious retreat amidst the vineyards of Château Smith Haut Lafitte. This five-star hotel and spa blend rustic charm with modern amenities, providing guests with an unparalleled experience of relaxation and indulgence. Prices for lodging at Les Sources de Caudalie start at €500 per night for a classic room, featuring chic decor and breathtaking views of the estate's grounds. Guests can unwind in the hotel's world-renowned spa, which offers a range of vinotherapy treatments inspired by the healing properties of grapes and wine. Unique to Les Sources de Caudalie is its gourmet restaurant, La Grand'Vigne, where guests can enjoy innovative cuisine paired with the finest wines from the region. Meal prices vary depending on the selected dining experience, with options available for both casual and fine dining. For reservations and inquiries, visitors can visit the official website at www.sources-caudalie.com.

Château de Mirambeau

Perched atop a hill overlooking the Gironde estuary, Château de Mirambeau offers a regal retreat steeped in history and elegance. Dating back to the 11th century, this magnificent château boasts beautifully appointed rooms and suites, each exuding old-world charm and sophistication. Prices for lodging at Château de Mirambeau start at €350 per night for a classic room, featuring antique furnishings and modern amenities. Guests can explore the château's manicured gardens, relax by the outdoor pool, or indulge in a game of tennis on the estate's private court. Unique to Château de Mirambeau is its gourmet restaurant, where guests can savor traditional French cuisine prepared with locally sourced ingredients. Meal prices vary depending on the selected menu, with options available for all tastes and preferences. For bookings and reservations, visitors can access the official website at www.chateaudemirambeau.com.

Château La Lagune

Located in the prestigious Haut-Médoc appellation, Château La Lagune offers guests the chance to experience life in a historic wine estate. Dating back to the 17th century, this charming château features elegantly appointed rooms and suites, each offering stunning views of the surrounding vineyards. Prices for lodging at Château La Lagune start at €300 per night for a standard room, featuring tasteful decor and modern amenities. Guests can explore the estate's vineyards, participate in wine tastings led by the château's winemakers, or simply relax in the tranquil surroundings. Unique to Château La Lagune is its gourmet picnic experience, where guests can enjoy a selection of local delicacies paired with the estate's wines amidst the beauty of the vineyards. Meal prices for this experience start at €50 per person. For reservations and inquiries, visitors can visit the official website at www.chateaulalagune.com.

Les Prés d'Eugénie

Situated in the picturesque village of Eugénie-les-Bains, Les Prés d'Eugénie offers guests a tranquil retreat in the heart of the French countryside. This Relais & Châteaux property features beautifully appointed rooms and suites, each elegantly decorated in a classic French style. Prices for lodging at Les Prés d'Eugénie start at €450 per night for a classic room, featuring luxurious amenities and views of the estate's gardens. Guests can indulge in a range of activities, including horseback riding, cycling, and fishing in the nearby river. Unique to Les Prés d'Eugénie is its world-class spa, where guests can unwind with a range of rejuvenating treatments inspired by the healing traditions of the region. Meal prices vary depending on the selected dining experience, with options available for both casual and fine dining. For bookings and reservations, visitors can access the official website at www.michelguerard.com.

Bordeaux's unique stays offer travelers the opportunity to immerse themselves in the region's rich history, culture, and natural beauty. From luxurious château accommodations to tranquil vineyard lodges, each establishment promises a memorable and enchanting experience that celebrates the essence of Bordeaux.

CHAPTER 3

TRANSPORTATION IN BORDEAUX

3.1 Public Transportation Overview

Exploring Bordeaux, a city known for its rich history, vibrant culture, and exquisite wine, is made convenient and accessible through its well-established public transportation system. Navigating this picturesque city is a breeze, thanks to a network of buses, trams, and river ferries that efficiently connect the various districts and attractions. Let's delve into the comprehensive overview of public transportation in Bordeaux, shedding light on the available systems, pricing, and tips for effective navigation.

Tram System: Bordeaux boasts one of the most extensive tram networks in France, renowned for its efficiency and accessibility. The sleek, modern trams glide through the city, offering passengers a comfortable and convenient mode of transportation. With four main lines crisscrossing the city and extending to the suburbs, travelers can easily reach key landmarks, such as Place de la Bourse, Quinconces, and the Bordeaux Saint-Jean train station. The tram system operates from early morning until late evening, providing frequent services to accommodate commuters and visitors alike.

Bus Network: Complementing the tram system is Bordeaux's comprehensive bus network, which serves areas not covered by the tram lines. With over 70 bus routes weaving through the city and its outskirts, passengers have access to a myriad of destinations, including residential neighborhoods, shopping centers, and cultural attractions. The buses run with regularity, ensuring minimal waiting times and efficient connections to other modes of transportation. Additionally, night buses cater to those traveling during the late hours, offering a reliable means of getting around after dark.

River Ferries: Adding a unique charm to Bordeaux's transportation network are its river ferries, which ply the Garonne River, providing scenic views of the city's waterfront. While primarily used for leisurely cruises, these ferries also offer practical transportation options for crossing the river. Visitors can hop aboard one of the BatCub ferries to reach destinations like the Cité du Vin or the Darwin Ecosystem on the opposite bank. The river ferries offer a refreshing alternative to traditional modes of transport, allowing passengers to soak in the beauty of Bordeaux's riverside architecture.

Bordeaux's public transportation system stands as a testament to the city's commitment to sustainable urban mobility and visitor convenience. With its efficient tram network, extensive bus routes, and charming river ferries, getting around Bordeaux is not only practical but also a delightful experience. By leveraging the integrated ticketing system and following navigational tips, travelers can effortlessly explore all that this enchanting city has to offer, from historic landmarks to culinary delights, ensuring a memorable journey through the heart of southwestern France.

3.2 Tram and Bus Services
Bordeaux's tram system stands as a hallmark of modern urban transportation, renowned for its efficiency and coverage. Comprising four

main lines labeled A, B, C, and D, the tram network spans across the city and extends into the suburbs, providing convenient access to key destinations. Line A, for instance, traverses from Mérignac to La Gardette, passing through major landmarks such as Place de la Bourse and the Saint-Jean train station. Each line is color-coded for easy identification, with sleek, modern trams running at frequent intervals throughout the day. Visitors can expect reliable service from early morning until late evening, making exploration of Bordeaux both convenient and accessible.

Bus Services in Bordeaux: Complementing the tram network is Bordeaux's extensive bus system, which serves areas beyond the reach of the tram lines. With over 70 bus routes crisscrossing the city and its outskirts, passengers have access to a plethora of destinations, including residential neighborhoods, commercial centers, and cultural attractions. The buses operate with regularity, ensuring minimal waiting times and efficient connections to other modes of transportation. Additionally, night buses cater to travelers venturing out during the late hours, providing a safe and convenient means of getting around after dark.

Ticketing and Pricing: Bordeaux's public transportation system offers a range of ticketing options to suit the diverse needs of travelers. Passengers can purchase tickets from vending machines located at tram stops, bus stations, and select retailers throughout the city. Single-ride tickets are ideal for one-off journeys, while day passes provide unlimited travel for a specified duration. For visitors planning an extended stay, multi-day passes offer cost-effective options to explore Bordeaux at leisure. Prices vary depending on the type of ticket and duration of validity, with discounted fares available for children, seniors, and persons with disabilities. The integrated ticketing system allows seamless transitions between tram and bus services using a single ticket, simplifying the travel experience for visitors.

Bordeaux's tram and bus services form the backbone of the city's public transportation network, offering efficient and accessible options for exploring its many attractions. With a comprehensive tram system covering the urban core and suburban areas, complemented by an extensive bus network reaching every corner of the city, visitors can navigate Bordeaux with ease. By leveraging the integrated ticketing system and following navigational tips, travelers can embark on a seamless journey through the heart of southwestern France, immersing themselves in the rich culture and history of Bordeaux.

3.3 Biking in Bordeaux

Bordeaux, with its charming streets, scenic riverfront, and historical landmarks, is a city best explored on two wheels. Cycling enthusiasts and casual riders alike can indulge in a variety of biking activities that showcase the city's beauty and cultural heritage. From leisurely rides along the riverbanks to exhilarating adventures through vineyard trails, Bordeaux offers a plethora of biking experiences to suit every preference.

Riverside Cycling on the Garonne River: One of the quintessential biking activities in Bordeaux is pedaling along the picturesque Garonne River. The Quai des Chartrons and Quai de Bacalan promenades offer dedicated bike lanes, inviting cyclists to leisurely pedal past historic buildings, lively cafes, and bustling markets. Visitors can rent bikes from numerous rental shops located near the riverfront or utilize the city's bike-share program, VCub, to embark on this scenic journey. Whether basking in the glow of the sunset or soaking in the riverside ambiance, cycling along the Garonne is an immersive experience that captures the essence of Bordeaux's waterfront culture.

Wine Tour by Bike in the Bordeaux Vineyards: For oenophiles and nature enthusiasts, a wine tour by bike through the Bordeaux vineyards is a must-do activity. Located just a short distance from the city center, renowned wine regions such as Saint-Émilion, Médoc, and Pessac-Léognan offer idyllic landscapes dotted with vineyards and châteaux. Cyclists can embark on guided or self-guided tours, meandering along scenic routes lined with vineyards, stopping to sample exquisite wines and savor gourmet cuisine at local wineries. The gentle terrain and refreshing countryside air make for an unforgettable biking experience, allowing visitors to immerse themselves in Bordeaux's rich winemaking heritage while enjoying the tranquility of the countryside.

Urban Exploration on Bordeaux's Bike Paths: Bordeaux's extensive network of bike paths makes it easy for visitors to explore the city's diverse neighborhoods and attractions on two wheels. From the bustling city center to the serene parks and green spaces, cyclists can traverse Bordeaux's urban landscape with ease. Notable bike-friendly areas include the historic district of Saint-Pierre, the verdant Jardin Public, and the vibrant Chartrons neighborhood. Rental shops and bike-sharing stations are conveniently located throughout the city, providing visitors with access to quality bikes and equipment. Whether navigating cobblestone streets or cruising along tree-lined boulevards, urban exploration by bike offers a unique perspective of Bordeaux's architectural marvels and cultural gems.

Mountain Biking in the Forests of Bordeaux: Adventure seekers craving adrenaline-fueled thrills will find solace in Bordeaux's surrounding forests and natural reserves, which offer exhilarating mountain biking opportunities. The pine forests of the Landes region and the rugged terrain of the Entre-Deux-Mers area provide scenic trails for riders of all skill levels. Cyclists can embark on guided tours or explore independently, tackling challenging ascents, technical descents, and winding singletracks amidst breathtaking scenery. With designated mountain biking areas such as the Domaine de Blanche-Fontaine and the Forêt de la Double, Bordeaux beckons outdoor enthusiasts to embrace the thrill of off-road cycling while discovering the region's natural beauty.

Cultural Heritage Cycling Tour: Delving into Bordeaux's rich history and cultural heritage, a cycling tour of the city's iconic landmarks and monuments offers a fascinating glimpse into its storied past. Visitors can pedal through the UNESCO-listed historic center, marveling at architectural treasures such as the Place de la Bourse, the Grand Théâtre, and the Cathedral Saint-André. Guided tours led by knowledgeable locals provide insights into Bordeaux's evolution from a medieval port city to a thriving cultural hub. Cycling past ancient churches, elegant squares, and charming alleyways, participants are transported through time, connecting with Bordeaux's legacy as a beacon of art, architecture, and savoir-faire.

Bordeaux's biking activities cater to a diverse range of interests, inviting visitors to explore the city and its surroundings from a unique perspective. Whether leisurely cycling along the riverbanks, embarking on a wine tour through vineyard trails, or immersing oneself in the city's cultural heritage, biking in Bordeaux promises unforgettable experiences. With accessible rental options, well-maintained bike paths, and a wealth of scenic routes to choose from, Bordeaux beckons travelers to embrace the freedom of two-wheeled exploration and discover the beauty and charm of this enchanting city.

3.4 Car Rentals and Taxis

For visitors seeking flexibility and autonomy in their exploration of Bordeaux and its surrounding regions, car rentals are an ideal choice. Several reputable car rental companies operate in Bordeaux, offering a diverse fleet of vehicles to cater to various preferences and budgets.

Europcar Bordeaux: With multiple locations throughout the city and at Bordeaux-Mérignac Airport, Europcar provides convenient access to rental vehicles for travelers arriving in Bordeaux. From compact cars for urban adventures to spacious SUVs for family excursions, Europcar offers a range of options to suit individual requirements. Visitors can book online through the company's website (www.europcar.com) or visit one of their branches to arrange a rental. Prices vary depending on the vehicle type, rental duration, and additional services.

Hertz Bordeaux: Hertz is another well-known car rental company with a presence in Bordeaux, offering a wide selection of vehicles and flexible rental terms. Travelers can find Hertz rental stations at strategic locations across the city, including Bordeaux-Saint-Jean train station and Bordeaux-Mérignac Airport. Booking can be done online via the company's website (www.hertz.com) or through their mobile app for added convenience. Prices are competitive and may vary based on factors such as vehicle category and rental duration.

Avis Bordeaux: Avis boasts a strong presence in Bordeaux, providing reliable rental services for both leisure and business travelers. With multiple rental locations scattered throughout the city, including downtown Bordeaux and Bordeaux-Mérignac Airport, Avis offers seamless access to rental vehicles. Customers can make reservations online through the company's website (www.avis.com) or by phone, choosing from a range of vehicle categories to suit their needs. Rental prices depend on factors such as vehicle type, rental period, and additional services requested.

Sixt Bordeaux: Sixt is a trusted name in the car rental industry, known for its diverse fleet and customer-centric approach. In Bordeaux, Sixt operates several rental branches, including locations at the airport and downtown areas. Travelers can browse and book rental vehicles through Sixt's user-friendly website (www.sixt.com) or mobile app, enjoying competitive rates and excellent service. Rental prices vary depending on the vehicle model, rental duration, and any optional extras selected.

Enterprise Bordeaux: Enterprise Rent-A-Car offers hassle-free car rental solutions for travelers exploring Bordeaux and its environs. With a focus on customer satisfaction and quality vehicles, Enterprise has established itself as a reliable choice for rental services. Visitors can easily reserve a vehicle online through the company's website (www.enterprise.com) or visit one of Enterprise's conveniently located branches in Bordeaux. Rental prices are competitive and may vary based on factors such as vehicle availability and rental duration.

Taxis in Bordeaux: For travelers seeking convenience and comfort without the responsibility of driving, taxis provide a reliable transportation option in Bordeaux. Licensed taxi services operate throughout the city, offering prompt pickups and professional service to passengers. When in need of a taxi in Bordeaux, travelers can hail one from designated taxi stands located at popular areas such as train stations, airports, and major tourist attractions. Additionally, taxi companies in Bordeaux provide phone booking services for advance reservations or on-demand pickups.

For visitors arriving at Bordeaux-Mérignac Airport, taxi services are readily available outside the terminal building, providing a convenient means of transportation to the city center and other destinations. While taxi fares in Bordeaux are metered, it's advisable to confirm the estimated fare with the driver before commencing the journey, especially for longer trips or journeys outside the city limits. Payment can be made in cash or by credit card, and tipping is not mandatory but appreciated for exceptional service.

Car rentals and taxis offer invaluable mobility solutions for visitors exploring Bordeaux and its surrounding regions. Whether opting for the freedom of driving your own vehicle or the convenience of hiring a taxi, travelers can expect reliable service and seamless transportation experiences in this vibrant French city. With a multitude of car rental companies and licensed taxi services to choose from, navigating Bordeaux is made effortless, allowing visitors to focus on enjoying the sights, sounds, and flavors of this enchanting destination.

3.5 Navigating Bordeaux on Foot

Bordeaux, with its rich history, stunning architecture, and vibrant culture, is best explored on foot, allowing visitors to immerse themselves in the city's charm and ambiance. From guided walking tours of historic neighborhoods to leisurely strolls along the riverbanks, Bordeaux offers a myriad of walking tours that cater to diverse interests and preferences.

Historic Walking Tour of Bordeaux's Old Town: Embark on a journey through time with a historic walking tour of Bordeaux's Old Town, a UNESCO World Heritage Site renowned for its architectural treasures. Led by knowledgeable guides, visitors can wander through narrow cobblestone streets lined with elegant 18th-century buildings, discovering hidden squares, medieval churches, and quaint boutiques along the way. Highlights of the tour include the iconic Place de la Bourse, the majestic Cathedral Saint-André, and the bustling Marché des Capucins. This tour provides insight into Bordeaux's rich history as a thriving port city and a center of trade and commerce.

Wine Tasting and Gastronomic Walking Tour: Delight your senses with a wine tasting and gastronomic walking tour, exploring Bordeaux's culinary delights and world-renowned wine culture. Led by local experts, this tour takes visitors on a gastronomic journey through the city's markets, bakeries, and wine bars, where they can sample delectable cheeses, pastries, and wines unique to the region. Stops may include the historic Chartrons district, known for its artisanal food shops, and the vibrant Saint-Pierre neighborhood, home to lively wine bars and restaurants. Along the way, participants learn about Bordeaux's culinary heritage and the art of food and wine pairing.

Art and Culture Walking Tour: Immerse yourself in Bordeaux's thriving art and cultural scene with a guided walking tour that highlights the city's museums, galleries, and public art installations. From the impressive collections at the Musée des Beaux-Arts to the contemporary exhibitions at the CAPC Museum of Contemporary Art, visitors can explore Bordeaux's diverse cultural landscape while admiring works by renowned artists past and present. The tour may also include stops at outdoor sculptures, street art murals, and historic landmarks that offer insight into Bordeaux's artistic heritage and creative spirit.

Green Spaces and Parks Walking Tour: Escape the hustle and bustle of the city and reconnect with nature on a walking tour of Bordeaux's lush green spaces and parks. From the expansive Jardin Public to the serene Parc Bordelais, visitors can wander through verdant gardens, shady promenades, and tranquil lakeshores, soaking in the beauty of Bordeaux's natural landscapes. Guided by local naturalists or park rangers, this tour offers opportunities for birdwatching, picnicking, and leisurely strolls amidst the city's urban oasis. Participants gain a deeper appreciation for Bordeaux's commitment to green urban planning and sustainable development.

Sunset Walk along the Garonne River: Experience the magic of Bordeaux at twilight with a sunset walk along the scenic Garonne River, where the city's historic waterfront comes alive in the golden glow of dusk. Starting from the iconic Place de la Bourse, visitors can stroll along the Quai de la Douane and Quai des Chartrons, pausing to admire panoramic views of the Pont de Pierre bridge and the majestic Porte Cailhau. As the sun sets over the river, casting a warm hue on the city skyline, participants can savor the romantic atmosphere and capture stunning photographs of Bordeaux's timeless beauty.

Exploring Bordeaux on foot offers a truly immersive and enriching experience, allowing visitors to discover the city's history, culture, and natural beauty at their own pace. Whether embarking on a historic walking tour of the Old Town, indulging in a wine tasting and gastronomic adventure, or simply enjoying a leisurely sunset stroll along the riverbanks, each tour offers a unique perspective on Bordeaux's charm and allure. With knowledgeable guides, scenic routes, and engaging activities, these walking tours promise unforgettable memories and a deeper understanding of Bordeaux's cultural heritage and vibrant spirit.

CHAPTER 4

TOP ATTRACTIONS/HIDDEN GEMS

Click the link or Scan QR Code with a device to view a comprehensive map of various Top Attractions in Bordeaux – https://shorturl.at/mnp1U

4.1 Iconic Landmarks: Bordeaux's UNESCO Sites

Bordeaux, a city steeped in history and adorned with architectural marvels, is home to several UNESCO World Heritage Sites that showcase its rich cultural heritage and significance. From grand squares and majestic cathedrals to sprawling urban landscapes, these iconic landmarks offer visitors a glimpse into Bordeaux's past and present.

Port of the Moon: Historic Bordeaux

Designated as a UNESCO World Heritage Site in 2007, the Port of the Moon (Port de la Lune) encompasses the historic center of Bordeaux, characterized by its crescent-shaped bend in the Garonne River. The site includes architectural masterpieces dating back to the 18th century, such as the Place de la Bourse, the Grand Théâtre, and the Palais Rohan. Visitors can explore the winding streets and picturesque squares of the Old Town, marveling at the well-preserved facades and intricate details of the buildings. The Port of the Moon is not only a testament to

Bordeaux's golden age of trade and commerce but also a vibrant cultural hub bustling with shops, cafes, and art galleries.

Saint-Émilion: Vineyard Landscape and Wine

Located just a short drive from Bordeaux, the picturesque village of Saint-Émilion is renowned for its vineyard landscape and winemaking heritage, earning it UNESCO World Heritage status in 1999. Nestled amidst rolling hills and lush vineyards, Saint-Émilion boasts charming cobblestone streets, ancient churches, and underground catacombs carved into the limestone cliffs. Visitors can embark on guided tours of the village's historic landmarks, including the Monolithic Church and the Saint-Émilion Collegiate Church, before indulging in wine tastings at local châteaux. The serene beauty and cultural richness of Saint-Émilion make it a must-visit destination for wine enthusiasts and history buffs alike.

Bordeaux, Port of the Moon: La Cité du Vin

La Cité du Vin, a futuristic cultural center dedicated to the history and heritage of wine, is a modern addition to Bordeaux's UNESCO World Heritage Sites. Opened in 2016, this iconic landmark offers immersive exhibitions, interactive displays, and tasting workshops that celebrate the art of winemaking and viticulture. Situated on the banks of the Garonne River, La Cité du Vin's striking architecture and panoramic views make it a captivating destination for visitors of all ages. From exploring the museum's vast collection of artifacts to sampling wines from around the world at the rooftop wine bar, a visit to La Cité du Vin promises an unforgettable sensory experience that highlights Bordeaux's enduring connection to wine culture.

Bordeaux, Port of the Moon: Saint-André Cathedral

Saint-André Cathedral, an architectural masterpiece dating back to the 11th century, is one of Bordeaux's most revered landmarks and a UNESCO World Heritage Site. Located in the heart of the city's historic center, the cathedral's Gothic façade and soaring bell towers dominate the skyline, offering a striking contrast to the surrounding medieval streets. Visitors can admire the intricate stone carvings and stained glass windows of the cathedral's interior, which tell stories of faith, art, and history. Ascending the cathedral's towers provides panoramic views of Bordeaux and the Garonne River, offering a unique perspective on the city's architectural heritage and urban landscape.

Bordeaux, Port of the Moon: Place de la Bourse

The Place de la Bourse, a grandiose square flanked by elegant palaces and reflecting pools, is a symbol of Bordeaux's prosperity and prestige as a center of commerce and culture. Designated as a UNESCO World Heritage Site as part of the Port of the Moon ensemble, the Place de la Bourse's neoclassical architecture and harmonious proportions attract visitors from around the world. Strolling through the square's sun-dappled promenade, visitors can admire the Fountain of the Three Graces, the majestic façade of the Palais de la Bourse, and the iconic Water Mirror, which reflects the surrounding buildings in mesmerizing patterns. Whether savoring a leisurely stroll or attending one of the many cultural events hosted in the square, a visit to the Place de la Bourse offers a captivating glimpse into Bordeaux's past and present.

Bordeaux's UNESCO World Heritage Sites is a journey through history, culture, and natural beauty that promises unforgettable experiences and discoveries. From the historic center of Bordeaux's Old Town to the picturesque vineyards of Saint-Émilion, each site offers a unique perspective on Bordeaux's rich heritage and enduring legacy. Whether marveling at architectural masterpieces, indulging in wine tastings, or simply soaking in the ambiance of a UNESCO-listed square, visitors are sure to be enchanted by the charm and allure of Bordeaux's iconic landmarks.

4.2 Off the Beaten Path: Hidden Gems

Bordeaux, known for its grand boulevards, historic landmarks, and renowned vineyards, also harbors a wealth of hidden gems waiting to be discovered by intrepid travelers. From secret gardens and quirky museums to lesser-known neighborhoods, these off-the-beaten-path destinations offer unique experiences and insights into Bordeaux's local culture and heritage.

Darwin Ecosystem: Urban Oasis of Creativity

Nestled along the Garonne River in the Bastide district, the Darwin Ecosystem is a vibrant hub of creativity, sustainability, and community activism. Housed in a former military barracks, this sprawling complex is home to artists' studios, organic cafes, urban farms, and eco-friendly businesses. Visitors can explore the site's graffiti-covered walls, repurposed shipping containers, and lush green spaces, soaking in the bohemian atmosphere and innovative spirit that define the Darwin Ecosystem. The site also hosts regular events, workshops, and cultural activities, making it a dynamic destination for those seeking alternative experiences in Bordeaux.

Les Bassins de Lumières: Immersive Digital Art Experience

Located in the Bassins à Flot district, Les Bassins de Lumières is a cutting-edge digital art center housed in a former submarine base. Utilizing state-of-the-art projection technology, the center transforms vast concrete chambers into immersive canvases for multimedia art installations. Visitors can wander through dimly lit corridors and cavernous halls, surrounded by mesmerizing projections of renowned artworks set to music and sound effects. The experience offers a captivating fusion of art, technology, and history, inviting visitors to explore the depths of their imagination in this subterranean sanctuary of creativity.

La Cité Frugès: Architectural Gem of Le Corbusier

Tucked away in the residential neighborhood of Pessac, La Cité Frugès is a hidden architectural gem designed by the renowned Swiss-French architect Le Corbusier. Built in the early 1920s as a prototype for affordable housing, the neighborhood features a series of colorful, cubist-style houses arranged around tree-lined streets and communal gardens. Visitors can take self-guided walking tours of the neighborhood, admiring the avant-garde architecture and innovative urban planning concepts that have influenced modernist design around the world. La Cité

Frugès offers a glimpse into the visionary ideas of Le Corbusier and the utopian aspirations of the early 20th-century architectural movement.

Les Vivres de l'Art: Cultural Playground in Bordeaux-Bastide

Les Vivres de l'Art is a dynamic cultural center housed in a former military warehouse in the Bordeaux-Bastide district. This eclectic space serves as a platform for contemporary art exhibitions, performances, workshops, and community events. Visitors can explore the center's industrial-chic galleries, outdoor sculpture garden, and rooftop terrace, which offers panoramic views of the city skyline. From avant-garde art installations to live music concerts and themed festivals, Les Vivres de l'Art fosters creativity, collaboration, and cultural exchange, making it a hidden gem worth discovering for art enthusiasts and curious travelers alike.

Parc Bordelais: Tranquil Retreat in the Heart of the City

Escape the hustle and bustle of the city and discover Parc Bordelais, a serene oasis of greenery and tranquility located in the heart of Bordeaux. Designed in the late 19th century by landscape architect Eugène Bühler, this expansive park features lush lawns, winding footpaths, and shaded groves, providing a peaceful retreat for locals and visitors alike. Visitors can enjoy leisurely picnics, scenic walks, and recreational activities such as boating on the park's picturesque lake or playing a game of pétanque under the canopy of old-growth trees. Parc Bordelais offers a welcome respite from urban life and a chance to reconnect with nature in the midst of Bordeaux's bustling streets.

Exploring Bordeaux's hidden gems off the beaten path offers a unique opportunity to uncover the city's lesser-known treasures and experience its local culture and creativity. From urban ecosystems and digital art centers to architectural marvels and tranquil parks, these destinations provide enriching experiences that complement the grandeur and charm of Bordeaux's more famous landmarks. Whether seeking artistic inspiration, architectural innovation, or simply a moment of tranquility amidst the urban landscape, these hidden gems invite visitors to venture off the tourist trail and discover the soul of Bordeaux.

4.3 Museums and Art Galleries

Bordeaux, a city renowned for its rich cultural heritage and artistic legacy, boasts a diverse array of museums and art galleries that offer immersive experiences for visitors. From classical masterpieces to contemporary creations, these iconic landmarks provide insights into Bordeaux's history, artistry, and cultural identity.

Musée d'Aquitaine: Gateway to Regional History

Located in the heart of Bordeaux's historic center, the Musée d'Aquitaine is a treasure trove of artifacts, documents, and artworks that trace the history of the Aquitaine region from prehistoric times to the present day. Housed in a magnificent 18th-century building, the museum's extensive collections include archaeological finds, medieval manuscripts, and ethnographic objects that shed light on Bordeaux's role as a crossroads of trade, culture, and civilization. Visitors can explore permanent exhibitions dedicated to topics such as Gallo-Roman civilization, the slave trade, and the French Revolution, as well as rotating temporary exhibitions that showcase diverse aspects of Aquitaine's cultural heritage. With its immersive displays, educational programs, and interactive workshops, the Musée d'Aquitaine offers a captivating journey through the region's past, making it a must-visit destination for history enthusiasts and curious travelers alike.

CAPC Museum of Contemporary Art: A Haven for Modern Art

Housed in a converted warehouse in the Chartrons district, the CAPC Museum of Contemporary Art is a dynamic institution dedicated to showcasing cutting-edge artworks from the 20th and 21st centuries. Founded in 1973, the museum's vast collection includes works by leading contemporary artists such as Andy Warhol, Anish Kapoor, and Louise Bourgeois, as well as emerging talents from around the world. Visitors can explore the museum's spacious galleries, which feature a diverse range of media including painting, sculpture, photography, and multimedia installations. In addition to its permanent collection, the CAPC hosts temporary exhibitions, artist residencies, and public programs that engage audiences with the latest trends and debates in contemporary art. With its innovative exhibitions, thought-provoking installations, and commitment to artistic experimentation, the CAPC Museum of Contemporary Art offers a stimulating cultural experience that appeals to art enthusiasts, scholars, and curious visitors of all ages.

Musée des Beaux-Arts: Masterpieces of Fine Art

Situated in the heart of Bordeaux's Golden Triangle, the Musée des Beaux-Arts is a prestigious institution renowned for its outstanding collection of European paintings, sculptures, and decorative arts spanning the medieval period to the 20th century. Housed in the former Hôtel de Ville, a magnificent neoclassical palace, the museum's galleries showcase works by renowned artists such as Rubens, Delacroix, and Renoir, as well as Flemish tapestries, Italian maiolica, and French porcelain. Visitors can admire masterpieces from the Renaissance, Baroque, and Romantic eras, as well as lesser-known gems from Bordeaux's local art scene. In addition to its permanent collection, the Musée des Beaux-Arts hosts temporary exhibitions, educational programs, and cultural events that celebrate the diversity and richness of European art history. With its opulent surroundings, world-class collections, and immersive exhibitions, the Musée des Beaux-Arts offers a captivating cultural experience that appeals to art lovers, history buffs, and connoisseurs of beauty.

Musée du Vin et du Négoce: A Journey through Bordeaux's Wine Culture

Located in the Chartrons district, the Musée du Vin et du Négoce offers a fascinating exploration of Bordeaux's wine culture, history, and commerce. Housed in a former wine merchant's mansion, the museum's exhibitions trace the evolution of winemaking techniques, trade routes, and tasting rituals that have shaped Bordeaux's reputation as a world-renowned wine capital. Visitors can explore immersive displays featuring vintage wine labels, cooperage tools, and historical artifacts related to Bordeaux's wine trade, as well as interactive installations that simulate the sensory experience of wine tasting and blending. In addition to its permanent collection, the Musée du Vin et du Négoce offers guided tours, wine tastings, and workshops that provide insights into Bordeaux's viticultural traditions and terroir. With its evocative ambiance, informative exhibits, and opportunities for hands-on learning, the museum offers a memorable journey through Bordeaux's vinous heritage that appeals to wine enthusiasts, connoisseurs, and curious travelers seeking to deepen their appreciation of the region's liquid treasures.

Musée Mer Marine: A Tribute to Maritime History

Set in a striking contemporary building on the banks of the Garonne River, the Musée Mer Marine is a maritime museum dedicated to preserving and celebrating Bordeaux's seafaring heritage. Opened in 2018, the museum's collections encompass a wide range of artifacts, models, and artworks that illustrate the history of navigation, exploration, and trade in the region. Visitors can explore galleries dedicated to topics such as shipbuilding, maritime commerce, and oceanography, as well as temporary exhibitions that highlight contemporary issues and innovations in marine science and technology. In addition to its permanent displays, the Musée Mer Marine offers educational programs, guided tours, and special events that engage visitors of all ages with the fascinating world of maritime history and culture. With its spectacular waterfront location, immersive exhibits, and diverse programming, the museum offers a captivating journey through Bordeaux's maritime past and present that appeals to history buffs, maritime enthusiasts, and families looking for enriching cultural experiences.

Exploring Bordeaux's museums and art galleries offers a rich tapestry of cultural experiences that celebrate the city's history, artistry, and identity. From ancient artifacts to contemporary creations, these iconic landmarks provide insights into Bordeaux's past, present, and future, inviting visitors to embark on a journey of discovery and appreciation. With their diverse collections, immersive exhibitions, and engaging programs, Bordeaux's museums and art galleries offer something for everyone, making them essential destinations for travelers seeking to explore the city's vibrant cultural landscape.

4.4 Parks and Gardens

Click the link or Scan QR Code with a device to view a comprehensive map of various Parks and Gardens in Bordeaux – https://shorturl.at/lyVW3

Located within the picturesque cityscape of Bordeaux are its verdant parks and gardens, each offering a serene retreat from the bustling urban life and a glimpse into the city's rich cultural heritage. These iconic landmarks not only provide a tranquil escape but also serve as living testaments to Bordeaux's commitment to preserving its natural beauty and historical legacy. From the lush greenery of Jardin Public to the enchanting Botanical Garden, Bordeaux's parks and gardens beckon visitors with their charm and allure, inviting them to embark on a journey of discovery and rejuvenation.

Jardin Public: A Verdant Oasis in the Heart of Bordeaux
Located in the heart of the city, Jardin Public stands as an emblem of Bordeaux's commitment to green spaces and public recreation. This sprawling park, spanning over 10 hectares, boasts meticulously

landscaped gardens, shimmering ponds, and shaded pathways, offering a tranquil respite amidst the urban hustle and bustle. Visitors can easily access the park by foot, bicycle, or public transportation, with several entrances conveniently scattered throughout the surrounding neighborhoods. One of the most notable features of Jardin Public is its historic botanical garden, dating back to the 18th century. Here, visitors can wander amidst an impressive collection of exotic plants and trees, carefully curated to showcase the diversity of flora from around the world. The garden also houses a charming carousel, delighting visitors of all ages with its whimsical allure.

Parc Bordelais: A Playground of Natural Beauty and Recreation

Situated in the northern part of Bordeaux, Parc Bordelais beckons visitors with its expansive green spaces, picturesque lakes, and family-friendly amenities. Spanning over 28 hectares, this idyllic park offers a perfect retreat for outdoor enthusiasts seeking relaxation and leisure activities. Parc Bordelais holds significant cultural value as a beloved community space, hosting various events and festivals throughout the year. From outdoor concerts to art exhibitions, the park serves as a vibrant hub of activity, fostering a sense of community and camaraderie among residents and visitors alike.

Jardin Botanique: A Horticultural Haven Amidst Urban Splendor

Tucked away in the heart of Bordeaux's historic center lies the enchanting Jardin Botanique, a hidden gem waiting to be discovered by botanical enthusiasts and nature lovers alike. This verdant oasis, spanning over four hectares, showcases a diverse collection of plant species from around the world, meticulously curated to educate and inspire visitors. Jardin Botanique holds significant historical and cultural significance as one of Bordeaux's oldest botanical gardens, dating back to the 18th century. Its rich heritage is reflected in its meticulously landscaped grounds, which feature rare and exotic plant species carefully cultivated over centuries.

Parc Floral: Where Nature Meets Artistry
Nestled within the charming neighborhood of Saint-Seurin, Parc Floral captivates visitors with its enchanting blend of natural beauty and artistic flair. This intimate botanical garden, spanning over three hectares, showcases a stunning array of plant species, complemented by whimsical sculptures and tranquil water features. Parc Floral holds significant cultural value as a hub of artistic expression, hosting various exhibitions and events throughout the year. From outdoor sculpture displays to botanical art workshops, the park serves as a vibrant canvas for creativity and inspiration, inviting visitors to explore the intersection of nature and art.

Parc Palmer: A Tranquil Haven in Bordeaux's Suburbs
Tucked away in the tranquil suburb of Cenon, Parc Palmer offers a peaceful retreat from the urban hustle and bustle, inviting visitors to reconnect with nature amidst lush greenery and serene water features. This expansive park, spanning over 17 hectares, boasts a diverse array of flora and fauna, making it a haven for outdoor enthusiasts and nature lovers alike. Parc Palmer holds significant cultural value as a cherished community space, hosting various events and activities throughout the year. From outdoor concerts to nature walks, the park offers something

for everyone to enjoy, fostering a sense of community and camaraderie among residents and visitors alike.

Bordeaux's parks and gardens stand as iconic landmarks, each offering a unique blend of natural beauty, cultural significance, and recreational opportunities. From the historic charm of Jardin Public to the artistic flair of Parc Floral, these green spaces invite visitors to embark on a journey of exploration and discovery, immersing themselves in the rich tapestry of Bordeaux's natural and cultural heritage. Whether it's a leisurely stroll amidst vibrant blooms or a family picnic by a tranquil pond, the city's parks and gardens offer a welcome respite from the urban hustle and bustle, beckoning visitors to linger awhile and savor the beauty that surrounds them.

4.5 Riverfront Exploration: Garonne River and Port of the Moon

Bordeaux's riverfront is a tapestry woven with history, culture, and natural beauty, where the Garonne River meanders through the heart of the city, offering a picturesque backdrop for exploration. From the iconic Port of the Moon to the bustling Quai des Chartrons, each landmark along the riverfront tells a story of Bordeaux's maritime heritage and vibrant waterfront culture, inviting visitors to embark on a journey of discovery and enchantment.

Port of the Moon: A UNESCO World Heritage Gem

Nestled along the banks of the Garonne River, the Port of the Moon stands as a testament to Bordeaux's illustrious maritime past and architectural splendor. Designated as a UNESCO World Heritage Site, this historic port district boasts a wealth of stunning landmarks, including the majestic Place de la Bourse, the iconic Water Mirror, and the imposing Porte Cailhau. Entry to most attractions within the Port of the Moon is free, although some may require a nominal fee for guided tours or special exhibitions. Whether it's admiring the grandeur of Place de la Bourse, strolling along the tranquil banks of the Garonne, or simply soaking in the ambiance of this UNESCO-listed treasure, the Port of the Moon offers a wealth of experiences for visitors to enjoy.

Quai des Chartrons: A Vibrant Riverside Hub

Located to the north of the city center, the Quai des Chartrons beckons visitors with its charming blend of historic architecture, trendy boutiques, and lively waterfront atmosphere. Once the bustling hub of Bordeaux's wine trade, this vibrant district now boasts a thriving arts and cultural scene, with galleries, cafes, and artisanal shops lining its picturesque quays. Entry to most attractions along the Quai des Chartrons is free, although some may charge a small fee for guided tours or special events. Whether it's browsing the eclectic galleries, sampling local delicacies at the bustling market, or simply taking in the sights and sounds of this dynamic riverside neighborhood, the Quai des Chartrons offers a vibrant tapestry of experiences for visitors to enjoy.

Pont de Pierre: A Symbol of Bordeaux's Connectivity

Spanning the Garonne River with its graceful arches and stately presence, the Pont de Pierre stands as a symbol of Bordeaux's enduring connectivity and architectural legacy. Built in the early 19th century by

Napoleon Bonaparte, this historic bridge offers stunning panoramic views of the city skyline and the surrounding riverbanks, making it a popular spot for photographers and sightseers alike. Entry to the Pont de Pierre is free for all visitors, making it an accessible destination for locals and tourists alike. Whether it's marveling at the bridge's elegant design, watching the sunset over the Garonne, or simply enjoying a leisurely stroll along its historic span, the Pont de Pierre offers a timeless glimpse into Bordeaux's rich heritage and natural beauty.

La Cité du Vin: A Wine Lover's Paradise

Perched on the banks of the Garonne River, La Cité du Vin stands as a beacon for wine enthusiasts and culture seekers alike, offering an immersive journey into the world of viticulture and viniculture. This architectural marvel, resembling a swirling wine decanter, houses a wealth of interactive exhibits, tasting rooms, and multimedia installations, inviting visitors to explore the rich history and cultural significance of wine. Entry to La Cité du Vin requires the purchase of a ticket, with various packages available to suit different interests and budgets. Whether it's sampling fine wines from around the world, learning about Bordeaux's winemaking traditions, or admiring the panoramic views from the rooftop observation deck, La Cité du Vin offers an unforgettable experience for wine lovers and curious minds alike.

CHAPTER 5

PRACTICAL INFORMATION AND TRAVEL RESOURCES

Click the link or Scan QR Code with a device to view a comprehensive map of Bordeaux – *https://shorturl.at/uIOY1*

5.1 Maps and Navigation

When embarking on a journey to discover the charms of Bordeaux, a city brimming with history, culture, and exquisite wine, one of the first steps towards a successful adventure lies in mastering the art of navigation. Whether you prefer the tactile experience of unfolding a traditional paper map or the convenience of digital platforms, Bordeaux offers a plethora of options to ensure you never lose your way amidst its winding streets and picturesque avenues.

Bordeaux Tourist Map: Unveiling the City's Treasures

For those enchanted by the romance of unfolding a tangible map, Bordeaux's tourist map serves as an indispensable companion. Widely available at tourist information centers, hotels, and various points of interest throughout the city, this meticulously crafted map unveils Bordeaux's treasures with intricate detail. From the majestic silhouette of the iconic Place de la Bourse to the quaint cobblestone lanes of the Saint-Pierre district, every corner of Bordeaux awaits exploration at your fingertips. With colorful illustrations highlighting key landmarks,

72

museums, parks, and gastronomic delights, the Bordeaux tourist map transcends mere navigation, serving as a gateway to immersive experiences. Whether you're tracing the path of the Garonne River or charting a course to the renowned wine estates of the surrounding countryside, this map is your trusted ally in unraveling Bordeaux's rich tapestry of attractions.

Digital Maps: Navigating Bordeaux in the Digital Age

In an era dominated by technology, Bordeaux embraces the digital revolution with open arms, offering a myriad of digital mapping solutions to cater to every traveler's preferences. From smartphone applications to online platforms, accessing Bordeaux's digital maps has never been easier or more intuitive. For the tech-savvy traveler, downloadable applications such as Google Maps, Citymapper, and Maps.me provide real-time navigation, transit information, and points of interest tailored to your preferences. Whether you're traversing Bordeaux's bustling streets on foot, navigating its efficient tram system, or embarking on a scenic bicycle ride along the riverbanks, these digital companions ensure seamless navigation at your fingertips.

Offline Access: Navigating Bordeaux Without Wi-Fi

For those seeking to disconnect from the digital realm and embrace a more traditional approach to navigation, Bordeaux offers ample opportunities to explore offline. Armed with a trusty paper map or a pre-downloaded digital map accessible without internet connection, you can wander freely through Bordeaux's enchanting streets without worrying about connectivity issues. Before setting out on your adventure, ensure you have the necessary offline maps downloaded to your device or secured a physical copy of Bordeaux's tourist map from one of the city's many distribution points. With offline access at your disposal, you can embark on impromptu explorations, venture off the beaten path, and immerse yourself in Bordeaux's hidden gems with confidence.

Comprehensive Digital Map: To further enhance your exploration of Bordeaux's myriad offerings, we invite you to access our comprehensive digital map, meticulously curated to showcase the city's wonders in all their glory. Simply click on the link or scan the QR code provided in this guidebook to access larger maps, including detailed descriptions of landmarks, curated itineraries, insider tips, and interactive features to tailor your experience to your preferences.

Whether you're a history buff yearning to delve into Bordeaux's storied past, a food enthusiast eager to sample the city's culinary delights, or a wine aficionado seeking to uncover the secrets of Bordeaux's prestigious vineyards, our digital map serves as your indispensable companion on this journey of discovery.

As you embark on your adventure through the enchanting streets of Bordeaux, mastering the art of navigation is essential to unlocking the city's myriad treasures. Whether you opt for the tactile experience of a traditional paper map or embrace the convenience of digital solutions, Bordeaux offers a wealth of options to ensure you navigate with ease and confidence. Armed with the knowledge imparted by this guide and equipped with the tools to explore Bordeaux's wonders, you're ready to embark on a journey filled with unforgettable experiences, cultural encounters, and moments of pure enchantment. So set forth with curiosity in your heart, and let Bordeaux reveal its secrets to you one discovery at a time.

5.2 Essential Packing List

Preparing for a visit to Bordeaux requires thoughtful consideration of the essentials to ensure a smooth and enjoyable journey. From versatile clothing options to practical accessories, here's a comprehensive guide to packing for your Bordeaux adventure.

Clothing: Versatility and Comfort

When it comes to clothing, versatility is key in Bordeaux's dynamic climate. As the city experiences mild winters and warm summers, pack a combination of lightweight, breathable fabrics for the warmer months and layerable pieces for cooler weather. A mix of t-shirts, lightweight sweaters, and a comfortable jacket or coat will ensure you're prepared for any temperature fluctuations. For exploring Bordeaux's cobblestone streets and vineyard trails, opt for comfortable walking shoes or sneakers that provide support and cushioning. Whether you're strolling through the historic city center or embarking on a wine tasting excursion, comfortable footwear is essential for enjoying all that Bordeaux has to offer.

Accessories: Practical Essentials

In addition to clothing, certain accessories can enhance your experience and provide convenience during your stay in Bordeaux. A sturdy daypack or tote bag is ideal for carrying essentials such as water bottles, sunscreen, and snacks while exploring the city or venturing into the countryside. Don't forget to pack a versatile scarf or shawl, which can serve as a stylish accessory for cool evenings or double as a picnic blanket for leisurely afternoons spent by the river. A compact umbrella or rain jacket is also advisable, as Bordeaux's weather can be unpredictable, especially during the shoulder seasons.

Technology: Stay Connected and Informed

In today's digital age, technology plays a crucial role in enhancing the travel experience. Ensure you pack essential gadgets such as a smartphone, camera, and portable charger to capture memories and stay connected with loved ones back home. A universal adapter is also essential for charging your devices, as electrical outlets in Bordeaux may differ from those in your home country. To navigate the city with ease, consider downloading offline maps and travel apps before your departure. These invaluable tools provide real-time information on public transportation, attractions, and dining options, ensuring you make the most of your time in Bordeaux without worrying about connectivity issues.

Health and Safety: Prioritize Wellness

Prioritizing your health and safety is paramount when traveling to any destination, and Bordeaux is no exception. Pack a small first aid kit containing essentials such as bandaids, pain relievers, and any necessary medications to address minor ailments or injuries during your trip. It's also advisable to carry a copy of your travel insurance documents and emergency contact information, should the need arise. Additionally, familiarize yourself with local emergency numbers and medical facilities in Bordeaux to ensure prompt assistance in case of an emergency.

Cultural Considerations: Respect and Courtesy

As you prepare for your visit to Bordeaux, take the time to familiarize yourself with local customs and cultural norms to show respect and courtesy to the residents of the city. While Bordeaux is known for its relaxed atmosphere and welcoming attitude towards visitors, observing basic etiquette such as greeting locals with a friendly "bonjour" and dressing modestly when visiting religious sites demonstrates cultural sensitivity and appreciation.

Packing for a visit to Bordeaux requires thoughtful consideration of the essentials to ensure a comfortable and enjoyable experience. By prioritizing versatility, practicality, and cultural sensitivity, you'll be well-equipped to navigate the city's charming streets, savor its culinary delights, and immerse yourself in its rich history and culture.

5.3 Visa Requirements and Entry Procedures

As an avid traveler and seasoned guidebook author, I recognize the pivotal role of detailed information in crafting a memorable journey. When planning your voyage to Bordeaux, a city brimming with culture and charm, understanding visa prerequisites and entry procedures is paramount for a hassle-free excursion.

Visa Requirements: Smooth Entry Assurance

Before setting foot in Bordeaux, it's essential to grasp the visa prerequisites according to your country of origin. Fortunately, for many travelers, Bordeaux lies within the Schengen Area, facilitating visa-free access for up to 90 days within a 180-day period for citizens of select countries. Nonetheless, it's imperative to ascertain whether your nationality mandates a Schengen visa or qualifies for visa-exempt status. Should a visa be necessary, ensure you initiate the application process well in advance of your intended departure. Consult your nearest French consulate or embassy for comprehensive guidance on visa application protocols and criteria.

Entry Procedures: Gateway to Bordeaux Unveiled

Upon arrival in Bordeaux, travelers are greeted with an array of transportation options to whisk them to the city center and commence their exploration. Whether by air, train, or road, each mode of transport offers its distinct allure and convenience.

By Air: Bordeaux's Aerial Portal

For visitors journeying from distant locales, Bordeaux-Mérignac Airport stands as the city's primary aerial gateway. Serving flights from major international hubs such as Paris, London, Amsterdam, and beyond, the airport offers seamless access to Bordeaux and its environs. Several airlines ply regular routes to Bordeaux-Mérignac Airport, offering travelers a diverse selection to cater to their preferences and budget. From legacy carriers like Air France and British Airways to budget-friendly options such as easyJet and Ryanair, a plethora of choices await those seeking passage to Bordeaux. For booking flights, explore the respective airlines' websites or reputable booking platforms to secure your ticket. Prices vary depending on factors like departure city, travel dates, and class of service.

- **Air France: Website** - airfrance.com. Prices for economy class typically range from $200 to $500, while business class fares start from $800 to $1500.
- **British Airways:** britishairways.com. Economy class fares range from $250 to $600, with business class tickets priced between $1000 and $2000.
- **easyJet:** easyjet.com. Economy class tickets are generally priced between $100 and $300, while business class options are not available.
- **Ryanair**: ryanair.com. Economy class fares range from $50 to $200, with no business class offerings available.

By Train: Bordeaux Unveiled by Rail

For travelers arriving from within France or neighboring European countries, the railway presents an efficient and picturesque means of reaching Bordeaux. The city is intricately linked to France's high-speed rail network, with frequent services traversing to and from destinations such as Paris, Lyon, and Toulouse. SNCF, France's national railway operator, manages domestic and international train services, encompassing high-speed TGV trains and regional TER trains. Tickets can be procured online via the SNCF website or authorized third-party platforms.

By Road: Bordeaux Awaits via Highway

For those preferring the freedom of road travel, Bordeaux is easily accessible by car through France's well-maintained highway system. Major routes such as the A10 and A62 connect Bordeaux to cities nationwide, making it a convenient option for travelers from neighboring regions or embarking on a European road trip. When driving to Bordeaux, acquaint yourself with French traffic regulations, including speed limits, toll roads, and parking guidelines. Consider factors such as fuel expenses, driving distances, and potential congestion when charting your course.

Navigating visa requirements and entry procedures to Bordeaux is an indispensable aspect of trip planning for any adventurer. By familiarizing yourself with visa stipulations, selecting the most suitable mode of transportation, and booking your travel arrangements in advance, you can ensure a seamless and fulfilling experience from the moment you arrive in this enchanting city. So prepare your documents, pack your bags, and embark on a voyage to Bordeaux, where a tapestry of discovery and wonder awaits your exploration.

5.4 Safety Tips and Emergency Contacts

Planning a visit to Bordeaux, the stunning city known for its wine, history, and architecture, can be an exhilarating experience. However, amidst the excitement, it's crucial to prioritize safety and be prepared for any unforeseen circumstances. Here are essential safety tips and emergency contacts to ensure a smooth and secure visit to Bordeaux.

Before You Go

Before embarking on your journey to Bordeaux, it's advisable to research the city's safety situation and any recent updates. Stay informed about current events and potential safety concerns by consulting reliable travel advisories from your country's government.

Packing Essentials

Pack your belongings wisely, including necessary medications, travel insurance documents, and a first-aid kit. Ensure that you have copies of important documents such as your passport, identification, and emergency contact information, both in physical and digital formats.

Getting Around Safely

While Bordeaux is generally a safe city, it's essential to remain vigilant, especially in crowded tourist areas and public transportation hubs. Keep an eye on your belongings at all times and beware of pickpockets. Utilize secure transportation options such as licensed taxis or reputable ride-sharing services, particularly during late hours.

Staying Connected

Stay connected with friends or family members back home by sharing your itinerary and updating them on your whereabouts regularly. Consider investing in a local SIM card or activating international roaming to ensure access to communication networks in case of emergencies.

Emergency Contacts

Familiarize yourself with essential emergency contacts in Bordeaux:

Police: In case of any criminal activity, emergencies, or incidents requiring police assistance, dial 17 for immediate help.

Medical Emergencies: For medical emergencies, including accidents or sudden illnesses, dial 15 to reach emergency medical services (SAMU). Bordeaux also has several hospitals and medical clinics equipped to handle various medical situations.

Fire Department: Dial 18 in case of fire emergencies or situations requiring assistance from the fire brigade.

Cultural Sensitivity and Respect: Respect the local customs, traditions, and cultural sensitivities during your visit to Bordeaux. Dress modestly when visiting religious sites, and be mindful of your behavior in public spaces. Learning a few basic phrases in French can also enhance your interactions with locals and show your respect for their language and culture.

Navigating the Nightlife: Bordeaux boasts a vibrant nightlife scene with numerous bars, clubs, and entertainment venues. While enjoying the nightlife, consume alcohol responsibly and avoid excessive drinking, which can impair your judgment and make you vulnerable to accidents or unwanted situations. Stick to well-lit and populated areas, especially when walking alone at night.

Natural Disasters and Weather Preparedness: Be aware of potential natural disasters such as floods or storms, especially if you're visiting Bordeaux during the rainy season. Stay informed about weather forecasts and heed any warnings issued by local authorities. If you encounter adverse weather conditions, seek shelter indoors and follow safety protocols.

A visit to Bordeaux promises unforgettable experiences, but prioritizing safety is paramount to ensure a memorable trip. By following these safety tips, staying informed, and being prepared for emergencies, you can explore Bordeaux with confidence and peace of mind, creating cherished memories that will last a lifetime.

5.5 Currency, Banking, Budgeting and Money Matters

When venturing into Bordeaux, being well-informed about currency exchange, banking services, and budgeting can significantly enhance your travel experience. Bordeaux, with its rich history and vibrant culture, offers a multitude of options to manage your finances effectively.

Currency Exchange

While the Euro (EUR) serves as the primary currency in Bordeaux, it's essential to acquaint yourself with the prevailing exchange rates. Several currency exchange bureaus dot the city, facilitating seamless transactions for visitors. From airports to major tourist hubs, these bureaus offer competitive rates for converting your currency into Euros. However, it's advisable to compare rates before committing to an exchange to ensure favorable deals.

Banking Services

Bordeaux boasts a diverse banking landscape, catering to both locals and tourists alike. Whether you need to withdraw cash, manage your finances, or seek financial advice, the city's banks provide a myriad of services to meet your requirements. Notable banks such as Société Générale, Crédit Agricole, BNP Paribas, Caisse d'Epargne, and La Banque Postale have established a strong presence in Bordeaux, offering a range of personalized banking solutions.

Société Générale

With multiple branches scattered across Bordeaux, Société Générale provides comprehensive banking services tailored to international visitors. From currency exchange to international money transfers, their proficient staff ensures hassle-free transactions. Whether you're a leisure traveler or a business professional, Société Générale's diverse range of financial products caters to your specific needs.

Crédit Agricole

Renowned for its customer-centric approach, Crédit Agricole extends a warm welcome to visitors seeking banking services in Bordeaux. Their branches, conveniently located throughout the city, offer multilingual assistance and a suite of banking solutions. Whether you require travel insurance or assistance with investment options, Crédit Agricole's knowledgeable staff provides expert guidance with a personal touch.

BNP Paribas

As one of the largest banking institutions in France, BNP Paribas ensures accessibility and convenience for visitors exploring Bordeaux. With innovative digital banking platforms and a network of ATMs, BNP Paribas simplifies financial transactions for travelers on the go. Additionally, their dedicated foreign exchange services cater to tourists requiring currency exchange facilities.

Caisse d'Epargne

Caisse d'Epargne stands out for its commitment to financial inclusion and customer satisfaction. With branches strategically situated in key locations across Bordeaux, they offer a wide array of banking products and services. Whether you seek budgeting advice or assistance with savings accounts, Caisse d'Epargne's attentive staff prioritizes your financial well-being.

La Banque Postale

Combining tradition with modernity, La Banque Postale embodies reliability and accessibility in Bordeaux's banking sector. With branches housed within post offices throughout the city, La Banque Postale caters to diverse clientele, including tourists requiring banking services during their stay. From basic account management to specialized financial solutions, their offerings resonate with visitors seeking simplicity and convenience.

Budgeting and Financial Tips

While indulging in Bordeaux's culinary delights and cultural attractions, prudent budgeting ensures a fulfilling experience without breaking the bank. Opting for local eateries and exploring free or discounted attractions can help stretch your budget further. Additionally, leveraging travel-friendly credit cards with low foreign transaction fees minimizes currency exchange expenses. Planning your itinerary in advance and setting aside a contingency fund for unforeseen expenses adds a layer of financial preparedness to your travel plans.

Bordeaux offers a wealth of resources to manage your finances effectively during your visit. From currency exchange bureaus to reputable banks with tailored services for tourists, the city ensures a seamless financial experience. By exercising prudence in budgeting and leveraging available resources wisely, you can fully immerse yourself in Bordeaux's charm while safeguarding your financial interests.

5.6 Language, Communication and Useful Phrases

Bordeaux, like much of France, primarily speaks French. While many locals, especially in tourist areas, may understand and speak some English, it's courteous and beneficial to learn a few basic French phrases to enhance your communication and immerse yourself in the local culture.

Basic Phrases

Learning simple phrases such as "Bonjour" (hello), "Merci" (thank you), "S'il vous plaît" (please), and "Excusez-moi" (excuse me) can go a long way in showing respect and fostering positive interactions with locals. Additionally, mastering basic numbers, directions, and common greetings can help facilitate everyday transactions and conversations.

Navigating Transactions

When dining out or shopping, it's common practice to greet the staff with a friendly "Bonjour" and to say "Merci" when receiving service. In restaurants, it's customary to wait for the waiter to bring the bill rather than asking for it directly. When paying, saying "L'addition, s'il vous plaît" (the bill, please) is polite and indicates that you're ready to settle the tab.

Asking for Assistance

If you find yourself in need of assistance or directions, approaching locals with a polite "Excusez-moi, parlez-vous anglais?" (Excuse me, do you speak English?) can help bridge any language barriers. Most people will appreciate your effort to communicate in French and will be more willing to assist you, even if they speak limited English.

Utilizing Translation Tools

For more complex conversations or situations where language barriers may pose a challenge, consider using translation apps or devices to facilitate communication. Apps like Google Translate allow you to translate text, speech, and even images in real-time, making it easier to convey your message accurately.

Cultural Sensitivity

In addition to language, understanding and respecting French cultural norms and etiquette can further enhance your communication and interactions in Bordeaux. For example, addressing people with "Monsieur" (Mr.), "Madame" (Mrs.), or "Mademoiselle" (Miss) followed by their last name is considered polite and respectful.

Engaging with Locals

Don't hesitate to engage with locals and immerse yourself in the vibrant culture of Bordeaux. Strike up conversations with shopkeepers, restaurant staff, or fellow travelers to learn more about the city's hidden gems, local traditions, and culinary delights. Showing genuine interest and respect for the local culture can lead to memorable experiences and meaningful connections.

Language and communication play vital roles in enhancing your experience during a visit to Bordeaux. By learning basic French phrases, respecting cultural norms, and utilizing translation tools when needed, you can navigate the city with confidence and forge genuine connections with locals. Embrace the opportunity to immerse yourself in the rich linguistic and cultural tapestry of Bordeaux, creating memories that will last a lifetime.

5.7 Useful Websites, Mobile Apps and Online Resources

Embarking on a journey to Bordeaux opens the door to a plethora of experiences, from savoring world-class wines to exploring historical landmarks. To enhance your visit and make the most of your time in this enchanting city, leveraging useful websites, mobile apps, and online resources is paramount. Here, we delve into five indispensable platforms tailored to enrich your Bordeaux experience.

Bordeaux Tourism Official Website

The Bordeaux Tourism Official Website serves as a comprehensive guide for visitors, offering a wealth of information on attractions, events, accommodations, and dining options. Navigating the website unveils insights into Bordeaux's rich cultural heritage, allowing you to craft personalized itineraries based on your interests. From wine tours to museum visits, the platform provides valuable resources to ensure a memorable stay in Bordeaux.

TripAdvisor

TripAdvisor emerges as a go-to platform for travelers seeking authentic reviews and recommendations. With an extensive database of user-generated content, TripAdvisor offers insights into hotels, restaurants, and attractions in Bordeaux. Whether you're scouting for top-rated eateries or hidden gems off the beaten path, the platform empowers you to make informed decisions, enhancing the quality of your travel experience.

Bordeaux Wine Official App

For wine enthusiasts venturing into Bordeaux, the Bordeaux Wine Official App proves indispensable. Designed to demystify the world of Bordeaux wines, the app provides access to vineyard tours, tasting notes, and wine-pairing recommendations. Additionally, it offers insights into

Bordeaux's esteemed wine appellations, allowing users to navigate the region's viticultural landscape with confidence and expertise.

Citymapper

Navigating Bordeaux's bustling streets and public transportation networks becomes effortless with Citymapper. This intuitive mobile app offers real-time transit information, including bus and tram schedules, route maps, and alternative transportation options. Whether you're exploring Bordeaux's historic center or venturing into its surrounding regions, Citymapper streamlines your travel experience, ensuring seamless navigation throughout your stay.

Bordeaux Expats Community Forum

For expatriates and international visitors seeking insider tips and local insights, the Bordeaux Expats Community Forum serves as a valuable online resource. Facilitating connections and exchanges among like-minded individuals, the forum fosters a sense of community while providing practical advice on navigating life in Bordeaux. From relocation assistance to cultural integration tips, the platform offers a supportive environment for newcomers to Bordeaux.

Leveraging useful websites, mobile apps, and online resources enhances your journey through Bordeaux, enriching your travel experience and facilitating seamless exploration. Whether you're immersing yourself in Bordeaux's cultural tapestry, indulging in its culinary delights, or embarking on wine-tasting adventures, these platforms serve as invaluable companions, guiding you every step of the way. By tapping into these resources, you unlock the full potential of your Bordeaux experience, creating cherished memories that endure long after your visit.

5.8 Visitor Centers and Tourist Assistance

Navigating the vibrant city of Bordeaux can be an enriching experience, filled with cultural discoveries and memorable encounters. To ensure a seamless visit, accessing visitor centers and tourist assistance services becomes paramount. These hubs serve as gateways to the city's treasures, offering invaluable resources and personalized assistance to enhance your exploration.

Visitor Centers

Bordeaux boasts several visitor centers strategically located across the city, each equipped to cater to the diverse needs of travelers. These centers serve as information hubs, providing insights into Bordeaux's attractions, events, accommodations, and transportation options. Whether you're seeking guidance on itinerary planning or assistance with booking tours, the knowledgeable staff at these visitor centers is poised to offer expert advice and recommendations tailored to your preferences.

Bordeaux Tourist Office - Centre

Situated in the heart of Bordeaux, the Bordeaux Tourist Office - Centre stands as a beacon for visitors seeking comprehensive assistance. With its central location on the Allées de Tourny, this visitor center offers multilingual support and a wealth of resources, including maps, brochures, and guided tour bookings. Whether you're exploring Bordeaux's UNESCO-listed urban ensemble or embarking on wine-tasting excursions, the Bordeaux Tourist Office - Centre serves as your trusted ally in navigating the city's offerings.

Bordeaux Tourist Office - Quinconces

Nestled within the iconic Place des Quinconces, the Bordeaux Tourist Office - Quinconces provides a convenient starting point for travelers venturing into Bordeaux's historic center. Boasting panoramic views of the Garonne River, this visitor center offers a picturesque backdrop as you gather information on sightseeing tours, cultural events, and dining experiences. With its prime location and dedicated staff, the Bordeaux Tourist Office - Quinconces ensures a warm welcome and seamless assistance for visitors exploring Bordeaux's treasures.

Bordeaux Tourist Office - Saint-Jean

Located near Bordeaux's main train station, the Bordeaux Tourist Office - Saint-Jean caters to travelers arriving by rail, offering immediate access to tourism services upon arrival. Whether you're embarking on a day trip to nearby vineyards or delving into Bordeaux's architectural marvels, this visitor center provides convenient support and guidance for your journey. From transportation inquiries to luggage storage facilities, the Bordeaux Tourist Office - Saint-Jean facilitates a smooth transition into your Bordeaux experience.

Bordeaux Metropole Tourist Office - Darwin

For travelers seeking a unique perspective on Bordeaux's cultural landscape, the Bordeaux Metropole Tourist Office - Darwin offers an alternative hub within the vibrant Darwin eco-district. Nestled amid converted military barracks, this visitor center embodies Bordeaux's spirit of innovation and sustainability. With its focus on eco-tourism initiatives and immersive experiences, the Bordeaux Metropole Tourist Office - Darwin provides enriching opportunities to explore Bordeaux's cultural heritage through a contemporary lens.

Bordeaux Wine Council - Maison du Vin

Enthusiasts embarking on wine-tasting adventures in Bordeaux find a haven at the Bordeaux Wine Council - Maison du Vin. Located in the heart of Bordeaux's historic district, this visitor center offers a gateway to the region's renowned vineyards and wine estates. From guided wine tours to tasting sessions led by certified sommeliers, the Bordeaux Wine Council - Maison du Vin invites visitors to indulge in Bordeaux's rich viticultural heritage while gaining insights into wine production techniques and terroir.

Bordeaux's visitor centers and tourist assistance services play a pivotal role in enhancing the travel experience, offering a wealth of resources and personalized guidance to visitors exploring the city's treasures. Whether you're seeking information on cultural attractions, culinary delights, or wine-tasting experiences, these hubs serve as invaluable allies, ensuring a memorable and enriching journey through Bordeaux. With their strategic locations and dedicated staff, Bordeaux's visitor centers stand ready to welcome and assist travelers, facilitating seamless exploration and discovery in this dynamic city.

CHAPTER 6
CULINARY DELIGHTS

6.1 French Local Dishes

Bordeaux, often renowned for its exquisite wines and breathtaking architecture, also holds a treasure trove of culinary delights waiting to be discovered. Nestled in the heart of southwestern France, Bordeaux boasts a rich gastronomic heritage that showcases the region's finest ingredients and culinary traditions. From savory classics to indulgent desserts, the city's diverse food scene offers a tantalizing experience for visitors seeking to immerse themselves in French cuisine. Let us embark on a gastronomic journey through five authentic French dishes that capture the essence of Bordeaux's culinary landscape.

Foie Gras: Indulgence Personified

One cannot delve into the culinary world of Bordeaux without indulging in the decadent pleasure of foie gras. Served as a delicacy in upscale restaurants and quaint bistros alike, foie gras embodies the essence of

French gastronomy with its rich, buttery texture and distinct flavor profile. Visitors can savor this exquisite dish at renowned establishments such as Le Chapon Fin or La Tupiña, where it is often accompanied by toasted brioche and a drizzle of sweet fruit compote. While prices may vary depending on the venue and presentation, expect to pay around €20 to €30 for a generous portion of this gastronomic delight. For an authentic experience, consider pairing foie gras with a glass of Sauternes, a sweet wine that complements its creamy texture perfectly.

Entrecôte Bordelaise: A Steak Lover's Paradise

For carnivores seeking culinary satisfaction, the entrecôte bordelaise stands as a testament to Bordeaux's love affair with beef. This classic dish features a succulent ribeye steak, grilled to perfection and adorned with a rich bordelaise sauce made from red wine, shallots, and bone marrow. Savored at traditional brasseries like Le Bouchon Bordelais or La Brasserie Bordelaise, the entrecôte bordelaise offers a symphony of flavors that will tantalize the taste buds of even the most discerning diners. Prices typically range from €25 to €35, depending on the cut and quality of the meat. To fully appreciate the dish's depth of flavor, pair it with a robust Bordeaux red wine, such as a Merlot or Cabernet Sauvignon, sourced from the region's esteemed vineyards.

Canelés: Sweet Temptations from Bordeaux

No culinary journey through Bordeaux would be complete without sampling the city's signature sweet treat - the canelé. These petite pastries, characterized by their caramelized crust and tender custard center, offer a delightful contrast of textures and flavors that captivate dessert enthusiasts worldwide. Visitors can indulge in canelés at local patisseries like Baillardran or La Toque Cuivrée, where these delectable confections are freshly baked to perfection. Priced at around €1 to €2 per piece, canelés serve as the perfect finale to any meal or as a delightful snack to enjoy while exploring the city's charming streets. For an authentic taste, be sure to savor these treats when they are still warm from the oven, allowing their flavors to meld together harmoniously.

Lamprey à la Bordelaise: A Unique Culinary Experience

Adventurous foodies seeking to expand their culinary horizons will delight in the opportunity to try lamprey à la bordelaise, a traditional dish that reflects Bordeaux's deep-rooted connection to its aquatic surroundings. This ancient recipe features lamprey, a jawless fish found in the waters of the Garonne River, cooked in a rich bordelaise sauce infused with red wine, garlic, and aromatic herbs. While not as commonly found on restaurant menus as other Bordeaux specialties, lamprey à la bordelaise can be enjoyed at select establishments like La Tupiña or Chez Jean-Mi, where it is revered for its bold flavors and unique culinary heritage. Prices for this specialty dish typically range from €30 to €40, reflecting both the rarity of the ingredient and the skill required to prepare it. For an unforgettable dining experience, pair lamprey à la bordelaise with a full-bodied Bordeaux wine, such as a Saint-Émilion or Pomerol, to accentuate its robust flavors and earthy undertones.

Garbure: A Hearty Taste of the Southwest

Rounding out our culinary journey is garbure, a rustic soup that epitomizes the warmth and conviviality of traditional French cuisine. Hailing from the Gascony region of southwestern France, garbure is a hearty stew made with an assortment of seasonal vegetables, cured meats, and flavorful broth. Served piping hot in cozy bistros like Le Petit Commerce or Le Plat à Oreilles, garbure offers a comforting and nourishing meal that is perfect for chilly evenings or leisurely lunches. Prices for a bowl of garbure typically range from €10 to €15, making it an affordable option for travelers looking to experience authentic French fare without breaking the bank. To enhance the dish's robust flavors, pair it with a crisp white wine from Bordeaux's Entre-Deux-Mers region, such as a Sauvignon Blanc or Semillon, which will complement its hearty ingredients and elevate the dining experience.

Bordeaux's culinary landscape is a tapestry of flavors, textures, and traditions that reflect the region's rich gastronomic heritage. From indulgent classics like foie gras and entrecôte bordelaise to unique specialties such as lamprey à la bordelaise and comforting dishes like garbure, visitors to Bordeaux are sure to be captivated by the city's culinary offerings. Whether savoring a leisurely meal at a Michelin-starred restaurant or sampling street food from a local market, every bite tells a story of tradition, innovation, and the enduring spirit of French cuisine. So come, immerse yourself in the culinary delights of Bordeaux, and embark on a gastronomic journey you won't soon forget.

Click the link or Scan QR Code with a device to view a comprehensive map of various Restaurants in Bordeaux – https://shorturl.at/opyDO

6.2 Restaurants and Cafés

Bordeaux boasts a vibrant culinary landscape that entices visitors with its blend of traditional French cuisine and innovative gastronomy. As one wanders through the charming streets adorned with historic architecture, the aroma of freshly baked bread and simmering sauces wafts through the air, beckoning hungry travelers to indulge in the city's diverse array of restaurants and cafes. In this gastronomic exploration, we delve into five establishments that epitomize Bordeaux's culinary excellence, each offering a unique culinary experience that tantalizes the senses and leaves a lasting impression.

Le Petit Commerce: A Haven for Seafood Enthusiasts
Located in the bustling Saint-Pierre district, Le Petit Commerce is a seafood lover's paradise, celebrated for its impeccably fresh catch and expertly prepared dishes. Situated near the Garonne River, this cozy bistro exudes a warm and inviting ambiance, with its rustic decor and friendly staff welcoming guests with open arms. The menu at Le Petit Commerce showcases an impressive selection of oysters, prawns, mussels, and other fruits de mer sourced directly from the nearby Atlantic

coast. Le Petit Commerce opens its doors daily from 12:00 PM to 3:00 PM for lunch and 7:00 PM to 10:30 PM for dinner, ensuring that seafood aficionados can indulge in their cravings throughout the day.

La Tupina: A Culinary Sanctuary for Rustic French Cuisine

Tucked away in the historic quarter of Saint-Pierre, La Tupina transports diners back in time to the rustic kitchens of rural France, where hearty, soul-satisfying fare reigns supreme. Housed within a charming 18th-century building adorned with wooden beams and vintage decor, this iconic restaurant exudes an air of timeless elegance, inviting guests to savor the flavors of tradition with every bite. To complement the rustic fare, La Tupina offers an extensive selection of wines from Bordeaux and beyond, allowing diners to discover the perfect pairing for their meal. La Tupina welcomes guests for lunch from 12:00 PM to 2:00 PM and for dinner from 7:30 PM to 10:30 PM, ensuring that patrons can indulge in an unforgettable culinary journey any time of day.

L'Alchimiste: Where Artistry Meets Cuisine

Nestled amidst the cobblestone streets of Bordeaux's historic center, L'Alchimiste captivates diners with its innovative approach to French cuisine, blending traditional techniques with modern flair to create culinary masterpieces that delight the palate and stimulate the senses. As guests step into this gastronomic haven, they are greeted by a chic and contemporary ambiance, with sleek furnishings and soft lighting setting the stage for an unforgettable dining experience. Led by acclaimed chef Julien Camdeborde, the kitchen at L'Alchimiste showcases a dynamic menu that highlights the finest seasonal ingredients sourced from local farmers and producers. L'Alchimiste welcomes guests for dinner from 7:00 PM to 11:00 PM, inviting them to embark on a culinary journey where artistry meets cuisine in perfect harmony.

Café Lavinal: A Charming Retreat in the Heart of Bordeaux

Nestled amidst the picturesque vineyards of the Bordeaux wine region, Café Lavinal offers a tranquil retreat where guests can unwind and savor the simple pleasures of life amidst breathtaking natural beauty. Located in the quaint village of Bages, just a short drive from Bordeaux city center, this charming café exudes rustic charm, with its ivy-clad facade and sun-dappled terrace providing the perfect setting for leisurely dining. Whether enjoying a leisurely brunch on the terrace or cozying up by the fireplace on a chilly evening, Café Lavinal welcomes guests with open arms, inviting them to experience the timeless charm of French countryside living. Open daily from 9:00 AM to 6:00 PM, Café Lavinal offers a serene escape where moments of bliss await around every corner.

Bordeaux's culinary scene offers a tantalizing array of flavors and experiences that captivate the senses and leave a lasting impression on visitors from near and far. From the seafood delights of Le Petit Commerce to the rustic charm of La Tupina, each establishment invites diners on a gastronomic journey through the rich tapestry of French cuisine, showcasing the region's bounty in every dish. Whether indulging in innovative fare at L'Alchimiste or savoring the tranquility of Café Lavinal, one thing is certain – a culinary odyssey in Bordeaux is an experience not to be missed, where every meal tells a story and every bite is a celebration of life's simple pleasures.

Click the link or Scan QR Code with a device to view a comprehensive map of various Bars and Pubs in Bordeaux – https://shorturl.at/gDMQ4

6.3 Bars and Pubs

From cozy neighborhood taverns to chic cocktail lounges, Bordeaux's bar scene offers something for every palate and preference. In this exploration, we uncover five establishments that epitomize the city's vibrant nightlife, each offering a unique ambiance and selection of libations to suit any mood or occasion.

Le Point Rouge: A Chic Wine Bar in the Heart of Bordeaux

Located in the bustling Saint-Pierre district, Le Point Rouge stands as a beacon of sophistication amidst Bordeaux's lively bar scene. Housed within a beautifully restored 18th-century building, this chic wine bar exudes an air of understated elegance, with its sleek furnishings and soft lighting providing the perfect backdrop for an evening of indulgence. Complementing the fine wines are an array of artisanal cheeses and charcuterie boards, showcasing the rich flavors of the region and providing the ideal accompaniment to a leisurely evening of sipping and savoring. Le Point Rouge welcomes patrons from 4:00 PM to midnight, inviting them to unwind and enjoy the finer things in life in the heart of Bordeaux.

The Connemara Irish Pub: A Lively Retreat for Guinness and Craic

Nestled along the bustling Quai de la Douane, The Connemara Irish Pub transports patrons across the Irish Sea to the lively streets of Dublin, where the sound of fiddles and laughter fills the air. Stepping into this cozy tavern, guests are greeted by the warm glow of dimly lit lanterns and the unmistakable aroma of hearty pub fare. From classic fish and chips to savory shepherd's pie, the pub's menu features an array of comforting dishes designed to satisfy even the heartiest of appetites. Open daily from 11:00 AM to 2:00 AM, The Connemara Irish Pub offers a spirited retreat where friends gather to raise a glass in celebration of life's simple pleasures.

La Comtesse Bar: A Glamorous Oasis of Art Deco Elegance

Perched atop the iconic Grand Hotel de Bordeaux, La Comtesse Bar beckons guests to experience the epitome of luxury and refinement amidst breathtaking panoramic views of the city skyline. With its opulent Art Deco decor and sophisticated ambiance, this glamorous rooftop bar sets the stage for an unforgettable evening of indulgence. La Comtesse Bar welcomes guests from 5:00 PM to 1:00 AM, inviting them to bask in the glow of Bordeaux's skyline while savoring the height of sophistication and style.

Frog & Rosbif: A Taste of England in the Heart of Bordeaux

Situated in the vibrant Saint-Pierre district, Frog & Rosbif offers a taste of England's pub culture amidst the charming streets of Bordeaux. With its cozy interior adorned with vintage memorabilia and traditional pub fare, this beloved watering hole exudes a warm and welcoming atmosphere, inviting guests to kick back, relax, and enjoy a pint or two. At Frog & Rosbif, patrons can choose from an impressive selection of craft beers brewed on-site, with options ranging from hoppy IPAs to rich stouts and refreshing lagers. Pairing perfectly with the brews are classic pub favorites such as hearty burgers, crispy fish and chips, and indulgent platters of loaded nachos, ensuring that hunger is never an issue for patrons looking to soak up the lively atmosphere

Bordeaux's bar scene offers a spirited tapestry of experiences, from chic wine bars and glamorous rooftop lounges to cozy neighborhood taverns and lively pubs. Whether seeking a taste of Bordeaux's world-renowned wines or a pint of Guinness amidst the company of friends, the city's diverse array of establishments provides something for every palate and preference. As night falls and the city comes alive with the buzz of laughter and clinking glasses, one thing is certain – a night out in Bordeaux is an experience to be savored and cherished, where every drink tells a story and every moment is a celebration of life's simple pleasures.

6.4 Cooking Classes and Workshops

Bordeaux, renowned for its exquisite wines and rich gastronomic heritage, offers visitors a unique opportunity to delve into the art of French cuisine through a variety of cooking classes and workshops. Nestled amidst the vineyards and historic streets of this vibrant city, these culinary experiences provide hands-on learning and immersion into the flavors and techniques that define Bordeaux's culinary identity. Let us embark on a journey to discover five exceptional cooking classes and workshops that showcase the best of Bordeaux's culinary scene.

L'Atelier des Chefs: Mastering French Cuisine with Expert Guidance

L'Atelier des Chefs, located in the heart of Bordeaux's city center, offers a range of cooking classes led by experienced chefs passionate about sharing their culinary expertise. From classic French dishes to modern interpretations, participants can choose from a variety of themes and techniques tailored to their skill level and interests. Prices for classes at L'Atelier des Chefs typically range from €50 to €100 per person, depending on the duration and complexity of the session. With small class sizes and personalized instruction, participants can expect to receive hands-on guidance and valuable insights into the art of French cooking. To make the most of the experience, visitors are advised to book in advance, as classes tend to fill up quickly, especially during peak tourist seasons.

La Cuisine Bordelaise: Discovering Regional Specialties in a Charming Setting

For those seeking to immerse themselves in the culinary traditions of Bordeaux and its surrounding region, La Cuisine Bordelaise offers an array of cooking classes focused on local specialties and seasonal ingredients. Located in a picturesque setting overlooking the Garonne River, this culinary school provides a tranquil and inspiring environment for participants to hone their cooking skills and deepen their understanding of Bordeaux's gastronomic heritage. Prices for classes at

La Cuisine Bordelaise start at around €80 per person and may vary depending on the menu and duration of the session. To enhance the experience, visitors can opt for add-ons such as wine pairings or guided market tours, providing additional insights into the region's culinary culture.

Cook'n With Class: Elevating Culinary Skills in a Dynamic Atmosphere

Cook'n With Class offers a dynamic and interactive approach to culinary education, with a focus on hands-on learning and creative expression. Located in the historic district of Bordeaux, this cooking school offers a diverse range of classes covering everything from traditional French cuisine to international flavors. Prices for classes at Cook'n With Class typically range from €70 to €150 per person, with options for private and group sessions available. Whether you're a novice cook or an experienced food enthusiast, the experienced chefs at Cook'n With Class will guide you through each step of the cooking process, ensuring a fun and rewarding experience for all participants. Visitors are encouraged to check the school's schedule regularly, as new classes and workshops are added frequently to accommodate varying interests and preferences.

Bordeaux Cooking School: Unleashing Creativity in the Kitchen

Bordeaux Cooking School, situated in a charming 18th-century building in the heart of the city, offers a range of cooking classes and workshops designed to inspire creativity and experimentation in the kitchen. Led by passionate chefs with a deep appreciation for local ingredients and culinary traditions, these sessions provide participants with the skills and confidence to create delicious dishes from scratch. Prices for classes at Bordeaux Cooking School start at around €60 per person and may vary depending on the menu and duration of the session. In addition to hands-on cooking instruction, participants can enjoy wine tastings and guided tours of nearby markets and artisanal food shops, providing a comprehensive understanding of Bordeaux's culinary landscape.

Le Foodist: Exploring the Cultural and Culinary Heritage of Bordeaux

Le Foodist offers a unique culinary experience that combines cooking classes with cultural immersion, allowing participants to discover the rich history and traditions of Bordeaux through its food and wine. Located in a beautifully restored townhouse in the city center, Le Foodist offers a range of classes and workshops focused on French cuisine and wine pairing. Prices for classes at Le Foodist start at around €90 per person and may vary depending on the theme and duration of the session. In addition to cooking instruction, participants can enjoy guided tastings of local wines and artisanal cheeses, providing a sensory journey through Bordeaux's culinary traditions. Visitors are encouraged to come with an open mind and a hearty appetite, as each class offers a feast for the senses and a deeper appreciation for the cultural richness of Bordeaux's culinary heritage.

Exploring the culinary delights of Bordeaux through cooking classes and workshops offers visitors a unique opportunity to connect with the region's rich gastronomic heritage and unleash their creativity in the kitchen. Whether mastering classic French recipes, discovering regional specialties, or exploring international flavors, these culinary experiences provide a memorable and rewarding way to immerse oneself in Bordeaux's vibrant food scene. With expert guidance from passionate chefs, hands-on learning opportunities, and a focus on local ingredients and traditions, cooking classes in Bordeaux offer something for every food enthusiast, ensuring a truly unforgettable culinary journey.

6.5 Wine Tasting Experiences

Bordeaux is renowned as one of the world's premier wine regions, celebrated for its exceptional terroir and diverse array of varietals. For wine enthusiasts and connoisseurs alike, embarking on a wine tasting journey through Bordeaux offers an unparalleled opportunity to explore the region's rich viticultural heritage and savor the nuances of its finest wines. Let us delve into five distinct wine tasting experiences that capture the essence of Bordeaux's winemaking traditions and showcase the diversity of its terroir.

Château Palmer: A Grand Cru Classé Experience

For a truly luxurious wine tasting experience, look no further than Château Palmer, a prestigious Grand Cru Classé estate located in the Margaux appellation. Set amidst manicured gardens and historic cellars, Château Palmer offers guided tours and tastings that provide insight into the estate's winemaking philosophy and heritage. Prices for tastings at Château Palmer start at around €50 per person and may vary depending on the selection of wines and the level of customization. Visitors are advised to book their tastings in advance, as availability may be limited, especially during peak tourist seasons. To enhance the experience, consider opting for a private tour or arranging a gourmet picnic amidst the vineyards, allowing you to fully immerse yourself in the splendor of Château Palmer's terroir.

La Cité du Vin: A Cultural and Sensory Journey

For an immersive wine tasting experience that combines education with entertainment, La Cité du Vin is a must-visit destination in Bordeaux. Located on the banks of the Garonne River, this architectural marvel houses a museum, exhibition spaces, and tasting rooms dedicated to the art and culture of wine. Visitors can choose from a variety of tasting workshops and thematic tastings that cater to different preferences and levels of expertise. Prices for tastings at La Cité du Vin start at around €20 per person and include access to the museum's exhibitions and multimedia experiences. To make the most of your visit, consider exploring the museum's interactive exhibits before or after your tasting, allowing you to deepen your understanding of wine and its significance in human history and culture.

Les Halles de Bacalan: A Gastronomic Wine Tasting Experience

For a taste of Bordeaux's vibrant culinary scene paired with exceptional wines, look no further than Les Halles de Bacalan, a bustling food market located in the city's revitalized Bacalan district. Here, visitors can sample a diverse selection of wines from local producers and vineyards while savoring gourmet delicacies from artisanal food stalls and eateries. Prices for wine tastings at Les Halles de Bacalan vary depending on the wines and the number of samples offered, with most tastings priced at around €10 to €20 per person. To fully appreciate the experience, take your time exploring the market's offerings, engaging with vendors, and indulging in regional specialties such as oysters, charcuterie, and cheese. Whether you're a seasoned wine enthusiast or a curious beginner, Les Halles de Bacalan offers a convivial atmosphere and a unique opportunity to discover the flavors of Bordeaux.

Château Pape Clément: Heritage and Tradition in a Historic Setting

For an authentic glimpse into Bordeaux's winemaking heritage, venture to Château Pape Clément, one of the oldest wine estates in the region with a history dating back over eight centuries. Located in the Pessac-Léognan appellation, this historic estate offers guided tours and tastings that allow visitors to explore its vineyards, cellars, and Renaissance-era château. Prices for tastings at Château Pape Clément start at around €30 per person and may vary depending on the selection of wines and the duration of the experience. To enhance your visit, consider joining a guided tour led by knowledgeable staff who can provide insight into the estate's history, winemaking techniques, and terroir. After your tasting, take a leisurely stroll through the estate's gardens or relax in the shade of ancient trees, reflecting on the timeless beauty and elegance of Château Pape Clément.

Bordeaux Wine School: Education and Exploration for Wine Enthusiasts

For those eager to deepen their knowledge of Bordeaux wines and terroir, Bordeaux Wine School offers a range of educational programs and tasting workshops designed to cater to enthusiasts of all levels. Located in the heart of Bordeaux, this renowned institution provides a comprehensive curriculum covering topics such as wine tasting techniques, grape varietals, and food and wine pairing. Prices for tastings and workshops at Bordeaux Wine School vary depending on the duration and level of the program, with introductory tastings starting at around €30 per person. To make the most of your experience, consider enrolling in a structured course or themed workshop that aligns with your interests and learning objectives. With expert guidance from certified sommeliers and educators, Bordeaux Wine School offers a dynamic and engaging learning environment that fosters a deeper appreciation for Bordeaux wines and the region's winemaking traditions.

Exploring the diverse wine tasting experiences of Bordeaux offers visitors a unique opportunity to immerse themselves in the region's rich viticultural heritage and savor the nuances of its finest wines. Whether indulging in a luxurious tasting at a Grand Cru Classé estate, embarking on a cultural journey at La Cité du Vin, or sampling gourmet delicacies at Les Halles de Bacalan, each experience promises to delight the senses and deepen your appreciation for Bordeaux's winemaking traditions. With a wealth of options to choose from, visitors can tailor their wine tasting itinerary to suit their preferences and interests, ensuring a memorable and rewarding journey through Bordeaux's wine country.

6.6 Food Markets and Local Specialties

Bordeaux beckons visitors with its rich culinary heritage and vibrant food markets brimming with local specialties. From artisanal cheeses to freshly caught seafood, these markets offer a feast for the senses and a glimpse into the gastronomic delights of the region. Let us embark on a culinary journey through five diverse food markets and local specialties that showcase the best of Bordeaux's culinary landscape.

Marché des Capucins: A Cornucopia of Flavors and Aromas

Located in the heart of Bordeaux's historic district, the Marché des Capucins stands as one of the city's oldest and most beloved food markets. Here, visitors can wander through aisles lined with stalls brimming with fresh produce, meats, cheeses, and gourmet delicacies sourced from local producers and artisans. Prices at the Marché des Capucins vary depending on the products and vendors, with affordable options available for budget-conscious travelers. To make the most of your visit, arrive early in the morning to experience the market at its liveliest and freshest, and be sure to sample specialties such as canelés, oysters, and regional wines as you explore.

Quai des Marques: Gourmet Delights Along the Garonne River

For a unique shopping experience with a picturesque backdrop, head to Quai des Marques, a waterfront promenade dotted with gourmet food stalls and artisanal shops overlooking the Garonne River. Here, visitors can browse a curated selection of local specialties, including cheeses, charcuterie, chocolates, and baked goods, while taking in panoramic views of the city's iconic bridges and historic architecture. Prices at Quai des Marques vary depending on the products and vendors, with options available for every budget. To enhance your visit, plan to arrive in the late afternoon or early evening, when the market comes alive with live music, street performers, and sunset views over the river.

Marché des Chartrons: A Haven for Foodies and Wine Enthusiasts

Situated in Bordeaux's trendy Chartrons neighborhood, the Marché des Chartrons offers a vibrant mix of food stalls, wine merchants, and artisanal boutiques showcasing the best of local and regional specialties. Here, visitors can sample a diverse array of products, from farm-fresh fruits and vegetables to homemade jams, sauces, and spices. Prices at the Marché des Chartrons vary depending on the products and vendors, with opportunities to taste and purchase wines from nearby vineyards at competitive prices. To avoid crowds, plan to visit the market on weekday mornings, when it is less busy, and be sure to explore the surrounding streets, which are home to charming cafes, restaurants, and wine bars.

Halles de Bacalan: A Culinary Playground in Bordeaux's Up-and-Coming District

For a taste of Bordeaux's culinary renaissance, venture to Halles de Bacalan, a modern food market housed in a renovated industrial warehouse in the city's up-and-coming Bacalan district. Here, visitors can discover a curated selection of gourmet products, including artisanal cheeses, charcuterie, seafood, and baked goods, sourced from local producers and vendors. Prices at Halles de Bacalan vary depending on the products and vendors, with options available for every budget. To fully immerse yourself in the experience, plan to visit on weekends, when the market hosts live cooking demonstrations, food festivals, and other culinary events that showcase the best of Bordeaux's gastronomic scene.

Marché de Saint-Michel: A Cultural and Culinary Gem in Bordeaux's Historic Quarter

Tucked away in Bordeaux's historic Saint-Michel neighborhood, the Marché de Saint-Michel offers a taste of old-world charm and authenticity amidst the city's bustling streets. Here, visitors can browse a diverse array of food stalls and specialty shops selling everything from local produce and meats to spices, herbs, and exotic delicacies from around the world. Prices at the Marché de Saint-Michel vary depending on the products and vendors, with affordable options available for every palate and budget. To experience the market at its liveliest, plan to visit on Sunday mornings, when locals gather to shop, socialize, and sample traditional dishes such as lamb confit, foie gras, and canelés.

Exploring the food markets and local specialties of Bordeaux offers visitors a unique opportunity to immerse themselves in the region's rich culinary heritage and discover the flavors that define its gastronomic identity. Whether wandering through the bustling aisles of the Marché des Capucins, savoring gourmet treats along the Garonne River at Quai des Marques, or indulging in farm-fresh delights at Halles de Bacalan, each market promises a memorable and rewarding experience for food lovers and adventurers alike. So come, explore the culinary bounty of Bordeaux, and embark on a gastronomic journey you won't soon forget.

CHAPTER 7

CULTURE AND HERITAGE

7.1 Bordeaux's Rich Cultural Heritage

Bordeaux, a city steeped in history and culture, offers a treasure trove of heritage sites that beckon visitors from around the globe. From majestic châteaux to quaint villages, each site whispers tales of bygone eras and preserves the essence of Bordeaux's rich legacy. Let us embark on a journey through Bordeaux's most captivating cultural heritage destinations, each offering a unique blend of history, art, and tradition.

La Cité du Vin: A Wine Lover's Paradise

Nestled on the banks of the Garonne River, La Cité du Vin stands as a beacon celebrating Bordeaux's renowned wine culture. With its striking architecture resembling a swirling wine decanter, this avant-garde museum invites visitors to embark on an immersive journey through the world of wine. While there is an entry fee, the experience is worth every penny, offering a captivating exploration of vineyards, winemaking traditions, and global wine heritage. Beyond its architectural marvels, La Cité du Vin holds profound cultural significance, serving as a testament to Bordeaux's centuries-old relationship with wine.

Saint-Émilion: A Medieval Marvel

Venture into the heart of Bordeaux's countryside, and you'll discover the enchanting village of Saint-Émilion. This UNESCO World Heritage site exudes medieval charm, with its labyrinthine streets, ancient churches, and sprawling vineyards. Saint-Émilion's historical significance dates back to Roman times, and its well-preserved architecture offers a glimpse into centuries past.

Musée d'Aquitaine: Unraveling the Tapestry of History

For those eager to delve into Bordeaux's multifaceted history, the Musée d'Aquitaine stands as a veritable treasure trove of artifacts and insights. Located in the heart of Bordeaux's historic district, this museum traces the region's evolution from prehistoric times to the present day. The Musée d'Aquitaine's collections span diverse eras and themes, encompassing everything from Gallo-Roman artifacts to contemporary art installations.

Basilique Saint-Michel: A Testament to Faith and Architecture

Dominating Bordeaux's skyline with its imposing spire, the Basilique Saint-Michel stands as a testament to both faith and architectural prowess. Dating back to the 14th century, this Gothic masterpiece beckons visitors with its soaring nave, intricately carved portals, and breathtaking stained glass windows. While entry to the basilica is free, donations are appreciated for its upkeep and restoration. Beyond its architectural splendor, the Basilique Saint-Michel holds profound cultural significance as a place of worship and pilgrimage.

Château de la Brede: A Noble Legacy

Journeying into Bordeaux's pastoral countryside, visitors will encounter the elegant Château de la Brede, once the ancestral home of renowned philosopher Montesquieu. This stately mansion, surrounded by manicured gardens and shimmering lakes, evokes the grandeur of France's aristocratic past. While there may be an entry fee for guided tours of the château and grounds, the experience is well worth it for history enthusiasts and admirers of French architecture. The Château de la Brede bears witness to Montesquieu's intellectual legacy, with its opulent salons and meticulously preserved library offering insight into the Enlightenment era.

Bordeaux's cultural heritage is a testament to the city's enduring legacy as a cradle of art, history, and tradition. From the vineyard-laden hillsides of Saint-Émilion to the grandeur of the Basilique Saint-Michel, each destination offers a captivating journey through time and culture. Whether you're a history buff, an art aficionado, or simply a curious traveler seeking new horizons, Bordeaux beckons with its myriad treasures waiting to be discovered.

7.2 Architectural Wonders: From Gothic to Contemporary

Bordeaux, a city renowned for its UNESCO-listed architectural ensemble, boasts a kaleidoscope of styles ranging from Gothic splendor to contemporary innovation. Each structure tells a story, weaving together the tapestry of Bordeaux's rich cultural heritage. Let us traverse through five architectural wonders, each offering a glimpse into the city's past, present, and future.

Basilique Saint-Michel: A Gothic Masterpiece

Standing proudly amidst the city's skyline, the Basilique Saint-Michel stands as a testament to Gothic grandeur. Its towering spire pierces the heavens, a beacon of faith and architectural prowess. Visitors are welcomed to explore this sacred sanctuary free of charge, though donations are appreciated for its ongoing preservation. Beyond its awe-inspiring façade, the Basilique Saint-Michel holds profound historical and cultural significance. Dating back to the 14th century, this architectural marvel has witnessed centuries of religious devotion and societal evolution. Inside, visitors can marvel at the intricate stone carvings adorning the nave, bask in the ethereal glow of stained glass windows, or ascend the Tour Pey-Berland for panoramic views of Bordeaux.

Cité Frugès-Le Corbusier: A Modernist Utopia

Venturing into Bordeaux's outskirts, visitors encounter the Cité Frugès-Le Corbusier, a living testament to modernist architecture. Designed by the legendary architect Le Corbusier in the early 20th century, this residential complex showcases the principles of functionalism and urban planning. Entry to the site is typically free, allowing visitors to wander through its geometric streets and contemplate the ideals of modern living. The Cité Frugès-Le Corbusier epitomizes the avant-garde spirit of the modernist movement, reflecting a vision of urban utopia rooted in simplicity and efficiency. Its cubist-inspired facades and minimalist design elements offer a stark contrast to Bordeaux's historic city center, yet harmonize seamlessly with the surrounding landscape. Visitors can explore the interior of select homes, attend architectural lectures, or simply stroll through the tranquil courtyards, pondering the enduring relevance of Le Corbusier's vision.

Palais Rohan: Baroque Splendor

Nestled along the banks of the Garonne River, the Palais Rohan enchants visitors with its opulent Baroque architecture. Built in the 18th century as the residence of the Archbishop of Bordeaux, this palatial edifice exudes regal grandeur and elegance. The Palais Rohan serves as a tangible link to Bordeaux's aristocratic past, bearing witness to centuries of political intrigue and cultural patronage. Its lavishly decorated salons, adorned with gilded moldings and ornate frescoes, offer a glimpse into the opulent lifestyle of the French nobility. Visitors can explore the palais's sumptuous interiors, attend classical concerts in its historic concert hall, or stroll through the meticulously landscaped gardens overlooking the river. Whether admiring the intricate details of its façade or contemplating the palace's storied past, the Palais Rohan promises a journey back in time to the height of Baroque splendor.

Darwin Ecosystem: Sustainable Innovation

In the heart of Bordeaux's industrial landscape, the Darwin Ecosystem emerges as a beacon of sustainable innovation and community engagement. Housed within a former military barracks, this dynamic complex serves as a hub for eco-friendly businesses, cultural initiatives, and urban regeneration projects. Entry to Darwin is typically free, fostering an inclusive atmosphere where visitors can explore, learn, and connect with like-minded individuals. Darwin represents a paradigm shift in urban development, prioritizing environmental stewardship, social cohesion, and economic resilience. Its repurposed warehouses and industrial spaces now house a vibrant mix of organic markets, art galleries, coworking spaces, and urban farms.

Grand Théâtre de Bordeaux: A Cultural Gem

Dominating Bordeaux's Place de la Comédie, the Grand Théâtre de Bordeaux stands as a monument to neoclassical elegance and artistic excellence. Built in the 18th century by architect Victor Louis, this architectural gem is renowned for its ornate façade, majestic Corinthian columns, and exquisite interior décor. The Grand Théâtre holds a special place in Bordeaux's cultural landscape, serving as a prestigious venue for opera, ballet, and classical music performances. Its lavish auditorium, adorned with glittering chandeliers and plush velvet seating, provides an enchanting setting for artistic expression and creative exploration. Bordeaux's architectural wonders offer a captivating journey through time, style, and innovation.

7.3 Performing Arts and Theater

Nestled within the heart of Bordeaux's cultural landscape lies a vibrant tapestry of performing arts and theatrical delights, each venue offering a unique blend of entertainment, enlightenment, and artistic expression. From historic theaters to contemporary performance spaces, Bordeaux's stage beckons visitors to immerse themselves in the magic of live performance. Let us embark on a journey through five of Bordeaux's most enchanting venues, each promising an unforgettable experience for theater aficionados and curious travelers alike.

Grand Théâtre de Bordeaux: Where Elegance Meets Excellence

Adorning the majestic Place de la Comédie, the Grand Théâtre de Bordeaux stands as a paragon of neoclassical elegance and artistic excellence. Designed by architect Victor Louis in the 18th century, this architectural gem serves as the city's premier venue for opera, ballet, and classical music performances. While tickets to performances may incur fees, visitors can admire the grandeur of the theater's exterior free of charge. The Grand Théâtre holds a storied place in Bordeaux's cultural heritage, having hosted illustrious performers and theatrical productions for centuries. Its opulent auditorium, adorned with gilded moldings and plush velvet seating, provides a sumptuous setting for artistic expression and creative exploration.

Théâtre National de Bordeaux en Aquitaine (TNBA): A Hub of Artistic Innovation

Located in the heart of Bordeaux's historic district, the Théâtre National de Bordeaux en Aquitaine (TNBA) stands as a beacon of artistic innovation and creative collaboration. Housed within a former Jesuit college dating back to the 17th century, this dynamic venue showcases a diverse array of contemporary theater, dance, and experimental performance art. While tickets to performances may have varying fees, the TNBA often hosts free events, workshops, and artist talks open to the public. The TNBA serves as a cultural nexus, fostering dialogue and exchange between artists, audiences, and communities. Its intimate theaters and rehearsal spaces provide a nurturing environment for emerging talents and established artists alike. Visitors can attend performances ranging from avant-garde theater to cutting-edge dance, participate in post-show discussions with artists, or explore the TNBA's vibrant program of workshops and masterclasses. Whether delving into the depths of experimental theater or savoring a classic Shakespearean drama, the TNBA invites visitors to engage with the transformative power of live performance.

Opéra National de Bordeaux: A Symphony of Sight and Sound

Tucked away in Bordeaux's historic Palais de la Bourse, the Opéra National de Bordeaux enchants audiences with its timeless blend of spectacle and sophistication. Founded in the 18th century, this prestigious opera house showcases a repertoire spanning opera, ballet, and symphonic concerts. While tickets to performances may have varying fees, visitors can often enjoy free recitals, open rehearsals, and behind-the-scenes tours. The Opéra National de Bordeaux holds a prestigious place in Bordeaux's cultural heritage, hosting world-renowned performers and innovative productions throughout its storied history. Its ornate auditorium, adorned with shimmering chandeliers and velvet draperies, provides a sumptuous backdrop for operatic grandeur and balletic grace.

Théâtre Fémina: A Gem of Belle Époque Glamour

Nestled along Bordeaux's bustling Cours Georges Clemenceau, the Théâtre Fémina exudes the charm and glamour of the Belle Époque era. Built in the early 20th century, this historic theater showcases a diverse program of theatrical productions, comedy shows, and musical performances. While tickets to performances may incur fees, visitors can appreciate the theater's exquisite Art Nouveau architecture and ornate interior décor. The Théâtre Fémina holds a special place in Bordeaux's cultural landscape, offering a platform for both established artists and emerging talents to shine. Its intimate auditorium, adorned with plush red seating and intricate gilt detailing, provides an inviting atmosphere for audiences to immerse themselves in the magic of live performance.

Le Rocher de Palmer: Where Diversity Thrives

Perched on the banks of the Garonne River in the suburb of Cenon, Le Rocher de Palmer stands as a testament to Bordeaux's vibrant cultural diversity and grassroots creativity. Housed within a converted quarry, this dynamic cultural center hosts a wide array of music concerts, theater performances, and community events. While tickets to concerts and performances may have varying fees, Le Rocher often hosts free exhibitions, workshops, and cultural festivals open to the public. Le Rocher de Palmer serves as a cultural melting pot, embracing a multiplicity of artistic genres and cultural influences. Its eclectic program features everything from world music and jazz to contemporary theater and experimental dance. Bordeaux's performing arts scene offers a kaleidoscopic array of experiences, each venue showcasing a unique blend of tradition, innovation, and artistic excellence. Whether reveling in the grandeur of the Grand Théâtre de Bordeaux or exploring the experimental realms of Le Rocher de Palmer, visitors are invited to embark on a journey through the transformative power of live performance.

7.4 Festivals and Events Calendar

Bordeaux, a city pulsating with life and culture, plays host to an array of vibrant festivals and events throughout the year, each offering a tantalizing glimpse into the city's rich tapestry of traditions, creativity, and community spirit. From wine celebrations to music extravaganzas, Bordeaux's calendar is brimming with experiences to delight every visitor. Let us delve into five of Bordeaux's most captivating festivals and events, each promising unforgettable moments and cherished memories.

Bordeaux Wine Festival: A Toast to Terroir and Tradition

Spanning the banks of the Garonne River, the Bordeaux Wine Festival stands as a grand celebration of the region's most prized export – its world-renowned wines. Held biennially along the quays of Bordeaux's historic waterfront, this spectacular event welcomes wine enthusiasts from around the globe to indulge in tastings, masterclasses, and cultural festivities. While certain activities may require tickets, the festival offers plenty of free entertainment for visitors to enjoy. The Bordeaux Wine Festival holds profound historical and cultural significance, paying homage to Bordeaux's centuries-old winemaking heritage and its esteemed position as the capital of wine. Visitors can meander through the festival's bustling wine pavilions, sampling vintages from prestigious châteaux and discovering hidden gems from local producers.

Bordeaux Fête le Fleuve: Celebrating the River's Rhythm

Every two years, Bordeaux Fête le Fleuve transforms the city's riverfront into a vibrant playground of maritime marvels and cultural revelry. This biennial event pays tribute to the Garonne River, the lifeblood of Bordeaux, with a dynamic program of nautical parades, water sports competitions, and riverside concerts. While entry to most activities is free, certain attractions may have ticketed access. Bordeaux Fête le Fleuve holds symbolic significance, honoring the city's historical ties to river commerce and maritime exploration.

Bordeaux International Arts Festival (FAB): A Tapestry of Creativity

Held annually in various venues across Bordeaux, the Bordeaux International Arts Festival (FAB) showcases a diverse program of contemporary performing arts, visual exhibitions, and interdisciplinary collaborations. While tickets to performances and exhibitions may incur fees, the festival also offers free outdoor performances, public installations, and artistic interventions throughout the city. FAB serves as a platform for cultural exchange and artistic experimentation, bringing together local and international artists to engage with audiences in innovative ways. Visitors can attend theater productions, dance performances, and multimedia installations in venues ranging from historic theaters to urban squares.

Bordeaux Métropole Street Art Fest: Where Urban Canvas Comes Alive

Embracing Bordeaux's vibrant street art scene, the Bordeaux Métropole Street Art Fest invites visitors to explore the city's hidden corners and overlooked spaces transformed into outdoor galleries. Held annually in different neighborhoods across Bordeaux, this grassroots festival celebrates urban creativity with a program of mural paintings, graffiti jams, and interactive street performances. Entry to most festival activities is free, allowing visitors to wander freely and discover artistic treasures around every corner. The Bordeaux Métropole Street Art Fest holds cultural significance as a catalyst for urban renewal and community engagement, transforming neglected urban spaces into vibrant hubs of artistic expression.

Bordeaux International Fireworks Festival: A Symphony of Light and Sound

Drawing visitors from near and far, the Bordeaux International Fireworks Festival illuminates the city's night sky with dazzling displays of pyrotechnic artistry and musical accompaniment. Held annually on summer evenings along the Garonne River, this beloved event showcases performances by renowned fireworks companies from around the world. While certain viewing areas may require tickets for optimal vantage points, the festival also offers free viewing zones along the riverbanks.

Bordeaux's festivals and events offer a kaleidoscopic array of experiences, each celebrating the city's cultural heritage, artistic diversity, and joie de vivre. Whether indulging in wine tastings at the Bordeaux Wine Festival, marveling at street art during the Bordeaux Métropole Street Art Fest, or witnessing the spectacle of fireworks at the International Fireworks Festival, visitors are invited to immerse themselves in the rhythm and revelry of Bordeaux's vibrant cultural scene. So come, join the festivities, and let Bordeaux's spirit of celebration ignite your senses and stir your soul.

7.5 Local Artisans and Craft Traditions

Nestled within the charming streets and historic quarters of Bordeaux, a treasure trove of local artisans awaits, each preserving centuries-old craft traditions and showcasing the timeless beauty of handmade goods. From artisanal chocolatiers to master craftsmen, Bordeaux's artisans offer visitors a unique opportunity to witness the magic of traditional craftsmanship firsthand. Let us embark on a journey through five of Bordeaux's most esteemed artisans and craft traditions, each weaving together the threads of history, culture, and creativity.

Bordeaux's Artisanal Chocolate Shops: Temptations of Sweet Delight
Scattered throughout Bordeaux's cobblestone streets, artisanal chocolate shops beckon visitors with the irresistible allure of handcrafted confections. From classic pralines to innovative flavor combinations, these chocolatiers showcase the artistry and passion that goes into every delectable creation. Bordeaux's artisanal chocolate shops hold both historical and cultural significance, reflecting the city's longstanding love affair with chocolate and confectionery craftsmanship. Visitors can embark on chocolate tasting tours, witnessing the meticulous process of

chocolate making from bean to bar and savoring the nuanced flavors of single-origin cacao.

Bordeaux's Ateliers de Céramique: Where Clay Comes to Life

Nestled within Bordeaux's artistic enclaves, ateliers de céramique invite visitors to witness the transformative power of clay in the hands of skilled artisans. From delicate porcelain tableware to sculptural works of art, these studios showcase the beauty and versatility of ceramic craftsmanship. Bordeaux's ateliers de céramique bear witness to the city's rich tradition of pottery and ceramics, dating back to Roman times. Visitors can enroll in pottery workshops, learning ancient techniques of hand-building and wheel-throwing under the guidance of experienced potters.

Bordeaux's Artisanal Perfumeries: Fragrances of Distinction

Amidst the bustling boulevards of Bordeaux, artisanal perfumeries entice visitors with the intoxicating scents of botanical essences and aromatic blends. From bespoke fragrances to artisanal soaps and candles, these perfumeries offer a sensory journey through the world of fine fragrance. Bordeaux's artisanal perfumeries carry on a legacy of perfumery craftsmanship that dates back to the Renaissance era. Visitors can participate in perfume-making workshops, concocting custom fragrances tailored to their preferences under the guidance of skilled perfumers.

Bordeaux's Artisanal Leather Ateliers: Craftsmanship in Every Stitch

Amidst Bordeaux's historic quarters, artisanal leather ateliers showcase the timeless art of leatherworking, where skilled craftsmen fashion fine leather goods by hand. From luxurious handbags to bespoke footwear, these ateliers epitomize the marriage of tradition and craftsmanship. Bordeaux's artisanal leather ateliers carry on a heritage of leatherworking that spans centuries, with the city once renowned for its tanneries and leather trade. Visitors can observe artisans at work, witnessing the meticulous process of leather cutting, stitching, and finishing.

Bordeaux's Artisanal Jewelry Boutiques: Adornments of Timeless Beauty

Scattered amidst Bordeaux's boutique-lined streets, artisanal jewelry boutiques showcase the exquisite craftsmanship and design innovation of local jewelers. From intricate metalwork to dazzling gemstones, these ateliers offer a treasure trove of adornments for every style and occasion. Purchasing handmade jewelry may require a financial investment.

Bordeaux's local artisans and craft traditions offer a window into the city's rich cultural heritage and creative spirit. Whether indulging in handmade chocolates, crafting ceramics, or selecting a bespoke fragrance, visitors are invited to immerse themselves in the artisanal traditions that have shaped Bordeaux's identity for centuries. So come, explore the ateliers and boutiques, and let Bordeaux's artisans inspire your senses and enrich your journey.

CHAPTER 8

OUTDOOR ACTIVITIES AND ADVENTURES

8.1 Exploring Bordeaux's Green Spaces

Nestled amidst the picturesque landscapes of southwestern France, Bordeaux beckons visitors with its lush green spaces and verdant parks. Beyond its famed vineyards and historic landmarks, the city boasts a plethora of outdoor adventures centered around its abundant natural beauty. Here, we delve into five captivating green spaces that promise unforgettable experiences for visitors seeking a breath of fresh air and a dose of tranquility.

Jardin Public: A Botanical Haven in the Heart of Bordeaux

Located in the heart of the city, Jardin Public stands as a tranquil oasis amidst the urban hustle and bustle. Open from dawn till dusk and free to enter, this historic park offers respite for weary travelers and locals alike. Accessible by foot, bike, or public transportation, including tram and bus, getting here is convenient for all. Steeped in history, Jardin Public dates back to the 18th century when it was designed by landscape architect Louis-Bernard Fischer. Its sprawling lawns, manicured gardens, and shimmering lake pay homage to Bordeaux's rich cultural heritage. Visitors can stroll along its shaded pathways, admire its diverse flora, or simply relax amidst its serene surroundings.

Parc Floral: A Burst of Color and Fragrance

Venture to the outskirts of Bordeaux, and you'll discover Parc Floral, a botanical marvel bursting with color and fragrance. Situated in the suburb of Lormont, this enchanting park welcomes visitors with open arms from sunrise to sunset, with no entry fee required. Travelers can easily reach Parc Floral by car, bike, or public transportation, making it an accessible destination for all. As you wander through its meticulously landscaped gardens, you'll encounter a dazzling array of flowers, shrubs, and trees from around the world. From vibrant roses to exotic orchids, the park's diverse flora delights the senses and provides a feast for the eyes. Visitors can also enjoy picnics, leisurely walks, or educational workshops amidst this botanical wonderland.

Parc Bordelais: A Green Haven for All Ages

Situated in the bustling neighborhood of Caudéran, Parc Bordelais beckons visitors with its expansive green spaces and family-friendly amenities. Open from dawn till dusk and free to enter, this beloved park offers something for everyone, from playgrounds and sports facilities to tranquil picnic areas. Accessible by foot, bike, or public transportation, including tram and bus, getting here is a breeze for all. Originally designed by landscape architect Eugène Bülher in the late 19th century, Parc Bordelais is steeped in history and cultural significance. Its majestic trees, meandering pathways, and charming pond pay homage to Bordeaux's rich heritage and commitment to preserving its natural beauty. Whether you're seeking outdoor recreation or simply seeking solace in nature, Parc Bordelais offers an idyllic retreat from the city's hustle and bustle.

Bois de Bordeaux: A Forested Sanctuary

For those craving a deeper immersion in nature, Bois de Bordeaux beckons with its vast expanse of woodlands and meandering trails. Located just a short drive from the city center, this sprawling forest offers endless opportunities for outdoor adventure, from hiking and biking to birdwatching and wildlife spotting. Open year-round and free to enter, Bois de Bordeaux invites visitors to explore its hidden treasures at their own pace. As you delve deeper into the forest, you'll encounter a diverse array of flora and fauna, including native oak, pine, and chestnut trees. Keep an eye out for deer, wild boar, and other wildlife that call this forest home. Whether you're seeking a leisurely stroll or a challenging hike, Bois de Bordeaux promises an unforgettable outdoor experience amidst the beauty of nature.

Parc aux Angéliques: A Riverside Retreat

Perched along the banks of the Garonne River, Parc aux Angéliques offers a scenic escape from the hustle and bustle of city life. Open from dawn till dusk and free to enter, this charming park welcomes visitors with its lush green lawns, shaded promenades, and panoramic views of the river. Accessible by foot, bike, or public transportation, including tram and bus, getting here is convenient for all. Named after the iconic angel statues that adorn its grounds, Parc aux Angéliques is steeped in history and cultural significance. Originally designed in the 18th century as part of Bordeaux's urban redevelopment, the park has evolved into a beloved gathering place for locals and tourists alike. Visitors can enjoy leisurely walks along the riverfront, picnics on the grassy lawns, or simply soak in the beauty of the surrounding landscape.

From historic parks to sprawling forests and scenic riverfronts, Bordeaux's green spaces offer a welcome respite from the hustle and bustle of city life. Whether you're seeking outdoor recreation, cultural enrichment, or simply a moment of tranquility, these verdant oases beckon with their beauty and charm. So pack your bags, lace up your walking shoes, and prepare to embark on an unforgettable journey through Bordeaux's lush landscapes.

8.2 Hiking and Nature Trails

Nestled in the heart of France's renowned wine country, Bordeaux isn't just about vineyards and cellars; it's also a paradise for nature enthusiasts and outdoor adventurers. Boasting a diverse landscape that ranges from lush forests to rolling hills, Bordeaux offers a plethora of hiking and nature trails that promise unforgettable experiences for visitors. Here, we delve into five captivating trails that showcase the region's natural beauty and cultural heritage.

Parc Bordelais: A Verdant Oasis in the City

Located in the heart of Bordeaux, Parc Bordelais serves as a green sanctuary amidst the urban hustle and bustle. Open from sunrise to sunset, this expansive park invites visitors to immerse themselves in nature's embrace at no entry fee. Accessible by public transportation, including tram and bus, getting here is a breeze for travelers and locals alike. As you wander along its winding paths, shaded by towering trees and adorned with vibrant flower beds, you'll discover the park's historical significance. Designed by renowned landscape architect Eugène Bülher in the late 19th century, Parc Bordelais is a testament to Bordeaux's rich cultural heritage. Beyond its lush landscapes, the park features playgrounds, sports facilities, and even a charming pond where visitors can relax and unwind.

Les Gorges du Verdon: A Natural Wonderland in Provence

Venture a bit further from Bordeaux, and you'll find yourself amidst the breathtaking beauty of Les Gorges du Verdon. Tucked away in the Provence-Alpes-Côte d'Azur region, this spectacular canyon offers a myriad of hiking trails that cater to all skill levels. From leisurely strolls along the riverbanks to adrenaline-pumping rock climbing adventures, there's something for everyone here. To reach Les Gorges du Verdon from Bordeaux, travelers can opt for a scenic drive or take advantage of organized tours. While there's no specific entry fee to access the canyon, visitors should be prepared for potential parking fees and equipment rental costs for certain activities. Once there, be sure to marvel at the sheer cliffs and turquoise waters that have earned Les Gorges du Verdon the title of "Europe's Grand Canyon."

Dune du Pilat: Scaling Europe's Tallest Sand Dune

For a truly unique outdoor adventure, look no further than Dune du Pilat, Europe's tallest sand dune. Situated along the Atlantic coast, just a short drive from Bordeaux, this natural wonder beckons visitors to conquer its towering heights and revel in panoramic views of the surrounding landscape. While there's no official opening or closing time, it's best to visit during daylight hours to fully appreciate its splendor. Accessing Dune du Pilat is relatively straightforward, with ample parking available nearby. While there's no entry fee, visitors should be prepared for a moderate climb up the dune's sandy slopes. Once at the summit, take a moment to catch your breath and soak in the awe-inspiring vistas of the Arcachon Bay and the lush pine forests beyond. Whether you're seeking adventure or simply seeking solace in nature, Dune du Pilat promises an unforgettable experience.

Sentier des Douaniers: Coastal Charms in Cap Ferret

Embark on a coastal adventure along the Sentier des Douaniers, a picturesque trail that winds its way along the rugged coastline of Cap Ferret. Named after the customs officers who once patrolled these shores, this trail offers breathtaking views of the Atlantic Ocean and the quaint fishing villages that dot the landscape. Open year-round, this trail is accessible to hikers of all abilities, with various access points along the coast. To reach Cap Ferret from Bordeaux, travelers can opt for a scenic drive or take a ferry across the bay. While there's no formal entry fee for accessing the trail, visitors should be mindful of any parking fees or transportation costs. Along the way, be sure to keep an eye out for local wildlife, including seabirds, seals, and even the occasional dolphin.

Whether you're craving a leisurely seaside stroll or a challenging coastal hike, the Sentier des Douaniers delivers an unforgettable outdoor experience.

Les Landes Forest: A Wilderness Retreat in Southern France

Escape the hustle and bustle of city life and immerse yourself in the tranquility of Les Landes Forest. Stretching across southwestern France, this sprawling forest offers endless opportunities for outdoor recreation, from hiking and mountain biking to birdwatching and picnicking. Open year-round and free to access, Les Landes Forest beckons visitors to explore its hidden wonders at their own pace. To reach Les Landes Forest from Bordeaux, travelers can embark on a scenic drive or take advantage of public transportation options. Once there, visitors can choose from a network of well-marked trails that meander through the forest's diverse ecosystems. Keep an eye out for native wildlife, including deer, wild boar, and the elusive European pine marten. Whether you're seeking adventure or simply seeking solace in nature, Les Landes Forest offers a welcome retreat from the everyday hustle and bustle.

From urban parks to coastal trails and ancient forests, Bordeaux offers a diverse array of outdoor adventures just waiting to be explored. Whether you're a seasoned hiker or a casual nature lover, there's something for everyone in this picturesque region of France.

8.3 Water Sports on the Garonne River

Along the banks of the majestic Garonne River, Bordeaux offers a playground for water sports enthusiasts seeking thrills and adventure.

From kayaking to stand-up paddleboarding, these exhilarating activities provide a unique perspective of the city's stunning waterfront. Here, we delve into five exciting water sports experiences that promise unforgettable moments on the Garonne.

Kayaking: Paddle Through Bordeaux's Historic Heart

Embark on a kayaking adventure and paddle your way through Bordeaux's historic heart, admiring iconic landmarks from the water. Several operators offer guided kayak tours along the Garonne, allowing visitors to explore the city's UNESCO-listed waterfront at their own pace. Tours typically last a few hours and cater to all skill levels, making them suitable for beginners and experienced paddlers alike. To access kayaking tours, visitors can head to the Quai Richelieu or Quai de Queyries, where many tour operators are based. While prices may vary depending on the duration and level of guidance provided, the experience of gliding past landmarks like the Place de la Bourse and Pont de Pierre is truly priceless. Whether you're a history buff or simply seeking an adrenaline rush, kayaking on the Garonne offers a unique perspective of Bordeaux's architectural wonders.

Stand-Up Paddleboarding: Glide Along the River's Surface

For a more leisurely water sports experience, try stand-up paddleboarding (SUP) on the Garonne River. With its calm waters and scenic views, the river provides the perfect setting for this increasingly popular activity. Whether you're a beginner or a seasoned SUP enthusiast, you'll find plenty to love about gliding along Bordeaux's waterfront on a paddleboard. Several rental shops along the riverbanks offer stand-up paddleboard hire, along with basic instruction for newcomers. Prices typically vary based on rental duration, with hourly and daily rates available. Once equipped with your paddleboard, set off from Quai des Chartrons or Quai de la Souys, and enjoy the freedom of exploring the river at your own pace. With the city's iconic skyline as your backdrop, stand-up paddleboarding on the Garonne promises moments of serenity and awe.

River Cruises: Explore Bordeaux's Waterways in Style

For those seeking a more relaxed water sports experience, consider a river cruise along the Garonne. Several companies offer guided boat tours that showcase the city's highlights from the comfort of a spacious vessel. From sunset cruises to wine-tasting excursions, there's a cruise to suit every taste and interest. To embark on a river cruise, head to the Quai de Chartrons or Quai Richelieu, where many tour operators have their docks. Prices vary depending on the duration and amenities included, with some cruises offering onboard dining and entertainment. As you glide along the Garonne, you'll pass by historic landmarks, lush vineyards, and picturesque countryside, providing a memorable glimpse into Bordeaux's rich cultural heritage.

Jet Skiing: Feel the Rush of Adrenaline on the Water

For adrenaline junkies craving high-speed thrills, jet skiing on the Garonne River offers an exhilarating experience like no other. Several rental companies provide jet ski hire, along with safety equipment and instruction for beginners. With the wind in your hair and the water beneath your feet, you'll feel a sense of freedom as you zip along the river's surface. To access jet ski rentals, head to designated rental stations along the riverbanks, such as Quai de Bacalan or Quai Louis XVIII. Prices typically vary based on rental duration and machine specifications, with options for solo riders or tandem passengers. Whether you're racing against the current or leisurely exploring the river's nooks and crannies, jet skiing on the Garonne promises an adrenaline-fueled adventure you won't soon forget.

Canoe Polo: Compete in a Unique Water Sport

For a truly unique water sports experience, consider trying your hand at canoe polo on the Garonne River. This fast-paced team sport combines elements of kayaking, basketball, and water polo, providing a thrilling challenge for participants of all ages and skill levels. Several clubs and organizations in Bordeaux host regular canoe polo sessions, welcoming newcomers to join in the fun. To participate in canoe polo, visitors can inquire with local clubs or organizations for information on training sessions and equipment rental. While prior experience in kayaking or canoeing is beneficial, beginners are also encouraged to give it a try under the guidance of experienced players. Whether you're competing in a friendly match or honing your skills in a training session, canoe polo offers a unique opportunity to bond with fellow enthusiasts while enjoying the beauty of the Garonne River.

From kayaking to stand-up paddleboarding and beyond, Bordeaux's water sports scene offers endless opportunities for adventure and exploration on the Garonne River. Whether you're seeking adrenaline-pumping thrills or tranquil moments of serenity, there's something for everyone to enjoy amidst the city's stunning waterfront. So pack your swimsuit, grab your paddle, and prepare to dive into an unforgettable aquatic adventure in Bordeaux.

8.4 Golf Courses and Outdoor Recreation

Nestled amidst the picturesque landscapes of southwestern France, Bordeaux offers a golfer's paradise with its lush green fairways and challenging courses. Beyond its renowned vineyards and historic landmarks, the city boasts a wealth of outdoor recreational opportunities centered around the sport of golf. Here, we delve into five captivating golf courses that promise unforgettable experiences for enthusiasts and novices alike.

Golf du Médoc Resort: Championship Golf Amidst Vineyards
Situated just a short drive from Bordeaux, Golf du Médoc Resort beckons golfers with its two prestigious 18-hole courses set amidst vineyards and pine forests. Designed by renowned architects Bill Coore and Rod Whitman, these championship courses offer a challenging yet scenic experience for players of all skill levels. The resort also features a driving range, putting green, and practice facilities for those looking to hone their skills. To access Golf du Médoc Resort, visitors can take a leisurely drive or arrange transportation through the resort's concierge service. While there is an entry fee to play the courses, guests can take advantage of special packages that include accommodation and dining options. Whether you're a serious golfer or simply seeking a leisurely round amidst breathtaking scenery, Golf du Médoc Resort promises an unforgettable experience.

Golf de Bordeaux-Lac: Urban Golfing at Its Finest

For golfers looking for convenience and accessibility, Golf de Bordeaux-Lac offers an urban oasis just minutes from the city center. This 18-hole course, nestled within the tranquil surroundings of Bordeaux's northern lakeside district, provides a welcome escape from the hustle and bustle of city life. With its well-manicured fairways and scenic water hazards, Golf de Bordeaux-Lac caters to players of all abilities. Accessing Golf de Bordeaux-Lac is easy, with ample parking available onsite and public transportation options nearby. While there is an entry fee to play the course, visitors can take advantage of special rates for twilight tee times or weekday play. Whether you're a local resident or a visitor to Bordeaux, Golf de Bordeaux-Lac offers a convenient and enjoyable outdoor recreation experience.

Golf de Teynac: A Hidden Gem in Bordeaux's Countryside

Escape the crowds and discover a hidden gem at Golf de Teynac, located in the scenic countryside just outside Bordeaux. This charming 9-hole course, set amidst rolling hills and wooded landscapes, offers a peaceful retreat for golfers seeking tranquility and natural beauty. With its relaxed atmosphere and friendly staff, Golf de Teynac welcomes players of all ages and abilities. To reach Golf de Teynac, visitors can take a short drive from Bordeaux or arrange transportation through the golf club's reception desk. While there is an entry fee to play the course, visitors can enjoy affordable rates and special discounts for groups and families. Whether you're a seasoned golfer or a beginner looking to improve your game,

Golf de Teynac offers a delightful outdoor recreation experience in Bordeaux's idyllic countryside.

Golf Blue Green Bordeaux-Lac: Lakeside Golfing with a View

Experience lakeside golfing with a view at Golf Blue Green Bordeaux-Lac, a scenic course overlooking the tranquil waters of the Bordeaux Lake. This 18-hole championship course, designed by renowned architect Jean-Claude Cornillot, offers a challenging yet enjoyable experience for golfers of all skill levels. With its panoramic vistas and pristine fairways, Golf Blue Green Bordeaux-Lac promises a memorable round in the heart of nature. To access Golf Blue Green Bordeaux-Lac, visitors can take advantage of the course's convenient location near the city center, with ample parking available onsite. While there is an entry fee to play the course, guests can take advantage of special offers and discounted rates for tee times booked in advance. Whether you're a serious golfer or simply seeking a leisurely day on the links, Golf Blue Green Bordeaux-Lac offers an unforgettable outdoor recreation experience.

Golf de Pessac: Historic Golfing Tradition in Bordeaux

Embrace Bordeaux's rich golfing tradition at Golf de Pessac, one of the oldest courses in the region with a history dating back to the 19th century. Nestled within a tranquil parkland setting, this 18-hole course offers a classic layout that challenges players of all abilities. With its well-maintained greens and scenic surroundings, Golf de Pessac provides a timeless golfing experience steeped in history and tradition.

To access Golf de Pessac, visitors can take a short drive from Bordeaux or arrange transportation through the club's reception desk. While there is an entry fee to play the course, guests can enjoy special rates for twilight tee times and weekday play. Whether you're a golfing enthusiast or simply curious to experience Bordeaux's golfing heritage, Golf de Pessac offers a memorable outdoor recreation experience for all.

8.5 Adventure Tours and Excursions

In the heart of southwestern France, Bordeaux isn't just a destination for wine enthusiasts and history buffs—it's also a playground for adventurers seeking thrilling experiences and unforgettable excursions. From soaring above the vineyards in a hot air balloon to exploring underground caves, Bordeaux offers a myriad of adventure tours and excursions that promise to ignite your sense of exploration. Here, we delve into exhilarating adventures that showcase the region's diverse landscapes and cultural heritage.

Hot Air Balloon Ride: Soar Above Bordeaux's Vineyards

Experience Bordeaux from a breathtaking perspective with a hot air balloon ride over its famed vineyards and countryside. As you gently ascend into the sky, you'll be treated to panoramic views of lush vineyards, historic châteaux, and picturesque villages below. The tranquility of the flight combined with the stunning scenery creates a truly magical experience that will leave you in awe of Bordeaux's beauty. Hot air balloon rides typically depart from designated launch sites in the Bordeaux region, such as Saint-Émilion or Médoc. Flights are usually scheduled in the early morning or late afternoon to take advantage of optimal weather conditions and favorable winds. While prices may vary depending on the duration and provider, the experience of drifting serenely above the landscape is well worth the investment.

Underground Cave Exploration: Discover Bordeaux's Hidden Depths

Delve into Bordeaux's rich geological history with an underground cave exploration tour that takes you beneath the surface of the earth. Guided by experienced spelunkers, you'll navigate through a labyrinth of subterranean passages, stalactites, and stalagmites, gaining insight into the region's geological formations and ancient history. From the eerie beauty of underground lakes to the mysterious depths of caverns, each cave offers a unique and unforgettable adventure. Several caves in the Bordeaux region are open to visitors, including the Grotte de Pair-non-Pair and the Grotte de la Devèze. Guided tours are typically available throughout the year, with varying levels of difficulty to accommodate different skill levels and interests. While some caves may charge an entry fee, the opportunity to explore these hidden treasures and witness the wonders of nature up close makes it a worthwhile investment.

Canoeing and Kayaking: Paddle Through Scenic Waterways

Embark on an aquatic adventure along Bordeaux's scenic waterways with a canoeing or kayaking excursion that promises thrills and exploration. Whether you prefer tranquil rivers or rushing rapids, there are options for paddlers of all skill levels to enjoy. Navigate through winding streams, past lush greenery and historic landmarks, and immerse yourself in the natural beauty of Bordeaux's waterways. Several tour operators offer guided canoeing and kayaking excursions on rivers such as the Dordogne, Garonne, and Isle. Tours typically include equipment rental, safety briefing, and knowledgeable guides who provide insights into the region's flora, fauna, and history. Prices vary depending on the duration and level of guidance provided, but the chance to paddle through Bordeaux's picturesque landscapes is an experience not to be missed.

Zip Line Adventure: Soar Through the Treetops
Experience the thrill of flight as you soar through the treetops on a zip line adventure in Bordeaux's scenic countryside. Strap into a harness, take a deep breath, and launch yourself into the air, zooming along steel cables suspended high above the ground. Feel the rush of adrenaline as you traverse through lush forests, over sparkling rivers, and past breathtaking vistas.

Several adventure parks in the Bordeaux region offer zip line courses with varying levels of difficulty and excitement. From family-friendly courses with gentle slopes to adrenaline-pumping challenges for daredevils, there's something for everyone to enjoy. While prices may vary depending on the park and course, the opportunity to experience Bordeaux's natural beauty from a unique perspective makes it a worthwhile adventure for thrill-seekers.

Horseback Riding: Explore Bordeaux's Countryside on Horseback

Saddle up and embark on a horseback riding adventure through Bordeaux's picturesque countryside, where rolling hills, vineyards, and historic landmarks await. Whether you're a seasoned equestrian or a novice rider, there are options for guided tours and excursions that cater to all skill levels and interests. Trot along scenic trails, canter through sun-dappled forests, and discover the timeless beauty of Bordeaux's rural landscapes.

Several equestrian centers and stables in the Bordeaux region offer guided horseback riding tours and lessons for visitors. Experienced guides lead riders on scenic routes that showcase the region's natural beauty and cultural heritage. Prices may vary depending on the duration and level of instruction, but the opportunity to connect with nature and explore Bordeaux's countryside on horseback is an experience that will leave a lasting impression.

CHAPTER 9

SHOPPING IN BORDEAUX

***Click the link or Scan QR Code with a device to view a comprehensive map of various Shopping Options in Bordeaux –
https://shorturl.at/ABD67***

9.1 Retail Therapy: Shopping Districts

Bordeaux, the vibrant city nestled in the heart of southwestern France, is not only renowned for its exquisite wines and picturesque landscapes but also for its diverse shopping districts that cater to every taste and preference. Embarking on a retail therapy journey in Bordeaux unveils a tapestry of experiences, each district offering its unique charm and selection of goods. Let's delve into captivating retail havens that epitomize Bordeaux's shopping scene.

Sainte-Catherine Street: The Pedestrian Paradise

At the heart of Bordeaux lies Sainte-Catherine Street, a bustling pedestrian thoroughfare adorned with elegant boutiques, chic cafes, and lively street performers. Stretching over 1.2 kilometers, it stands as one of Europe's longest shopping streets, attracting locals and tourists alike. Here, fashion aficionados can revel in a plethora of offerings, from haute couture to trendy streetwear. Luxury brands like Louis Vuitton and Chanel share the spotlight with high-street favorites like Zara and H&M.

Additionally, quaint artisanal shops showcase locally crafted jewelry, leather goods, and artwork, adding a touch of authenticity to the shopping experience. Prices vary depending on the brand and product, catering to diverse budgets. Sainte-Catherine Street comes to life from 10:00 AM to 8:00 PM, with some stores closing for a siesta between 1:00 PM and 3:00 PM. Conveniently located in the city center, accessing Sainte-Catherine Street is effortless via tram, with stops at Place de la Comédie and Quinconces.

Les Grands Hommes: Luxury and Elegance

For those seeking a taste of luxury, Les Grands Hommes emerges as Bordeaux's premier destination. Situated in the Golden Triangle, this upscale district exudes opulence with its grand architecture and exclusive boutiques. Renowned fashion houses such as Dior, Hermès, and Gucci line the boulevards, enticing shoppers with their exquisite collections of apparel, accessories, and perfumes. The ambiance is sophisticated, catering to discerning clientele with a penchant for refinement. While prices reflect the premium quality of goods, Les Grands Hommes also offers mid-range options for those seeking a touch of luxury without breaking the bank. Operating hours typically range from 10:00 AM to 7:00 PM, with variations among individual stores. Accessing Les Grands Hommes is convenient, as it lies within walking distance from the city center or can be reached via tram, with the Grand Théâtre stop being the closest.

Capucins Market: A Gastronomic Delight

Beyond fashion, Bordeaux beckons food enthusiasts to indulge in its culinary treasures at the Capucins Market. Nestled in the historic district of Saint-Michel, this bustling market has been a culinary hub since the 18th century, offering an array of fresh produce, gourmet delicacies, and regional specialties. Visitors can immerse themselves in a sensory feast as they meander through stalls brimming with colorful fruits, fragrant cheeses, and succulent seafood. Artisanal bakeries tempt with crusty baguettes and delicate pastries, while cozy cafes beckon for a leisurely espresso break. Prices at Capucins Market are reasonable, allowing visitors to savor Bordeaux's gastronomic delights without breaking the bank. The market operates from Tuesday to Sunday, with varying hours depending on the day. It opens early, typically around 6:00 AM, and winds down by mid-afternoon. Accessing Capucins Market is convenient via tram, with the Saint-Michel stop located nearby, or by foot from the city center.

Quartier des Chartrons: Vintage Chic and Artisanal Finds

In the picturesque Quartier des Chartrons, history and creativity converge to offer a unique shopping experience brimming with vintage charm and artisanal flair. Once the epicenter of Bordeaux's wine trade, this quaint neighborhood now hosts an eclectic mix of antique shops, art galleries, and concept stores. Visitors can unearth hidden treasures as they browse through vintage clothing, retro furniture, and one-of-a-kind artworks. Local artisans showcase their craftsmanship, offering handmade jewelry, ceramics, and home décor items imbued with a distinct Bordeaux charm. Prices in Quartier des Chartrons vary depending on the rarity and craftsmanship of the goods, with options to suit every budget. Most shops operate from 10:00 AM to 7:00 PM, with slight variations among establishments. Accessing Quartier des Chartrons is convenient via tram, with stops at Chartrons or Cours du Médoc, or by a leisurely stroll along the Garonne River from the city center.

Rue Notre-Dame: Quaint Boutiques and Hidden Gems

Tucked away from the bustling city center, Rue Notre-Dame invites visitors to wander through its picturesque streets lined with charming boutiques and hidden gems waiting to be discovered. This eclectic neighborhood exudes a laid-back ambiance, offering a delightful escape from the urban hustle. Visitors can peruse a curated selection of independent shops showcasing unique fashion finds, artisanal crafts, and gourmet treats. From stylish boutiques offering locally designed clothing to quaint bookshops brimming with literary treasures, Rue Notre-Dame caters to a diverse range of tastes. Prices here are often reasonable, with opportunities to snag authentic Bordeaux souvenirs and gifts at affordable prices. Operating hours vary among establishments, typically ranging from 10:00 AM to 7:00 PM. Accessing Rue Notre-Dame is straightforward, either by tram to Place du Palais or by a leisurely walk from the city center, allowing visitors to soak in the neighborhood's quaint charm along the way.

Bordeaux's diverse shopping districts offer a tapestry of experiences, each imbued with its unique charm and selection of goods. Whether indulging in luxury fashion, savoring gastronomic delights, or uncovering vintage treasures, visitors are sure to find their retail haven amidst

Bordeaux's vibrant streets. With convenient access via tram and a plethora of options to suit every budget and taste, embarking on a retail therapy journey in Bordeaux is an unforgettable experience that promises to delight the senses and satisfy the soul.

9.2 Boutiques and Designer Stores

Bordeaux, the epitome of elegance and sophistication, beckons visitors to explore its array of boutiques and designer stores that showcase the finest in fashion and luxury. Nestled amidst the charming streets of this historic city are five distinct establishments, each offering a curated selection of goods and a unique shopping experience.

Le Chic Parisien: Parisian Flair in Bordeaux

Located in the heart of Bordeaux's city center, Le Chic Parisien exudes quintessential Parisian charm with its elegant storefront and chic interior. This boutique specializes in luxury women's fashion, offering a curated selection of designer clothing, handbags, and accessories. From timeless pieces by Chanel and Dior to contemporary designs by Isabel Marant and Chloé, Le Chic Parisien caters to discerning clientele seeking sophisticated style. Prices at Le Chic Parisien reflect the premium quality and craftsmanship of the goods, with dresses ranging from €300 to €2000 and handbags starting at €500. The boutique opens its doors from 10:00 AM to 7:00 PM, providing ample time for a leisurely shopping experience. Accessing Le Chic Parisien is convenient, as it is situated near the city's main tram lines, with stops at Gambetta and Grand Théâtre.

La Maison du Luxe: A Haven for High-End Fashion

Nestled in the prestigious Golden Triangle, La Maison du Luxe stands as a beacon of luxury amidst Bordeaux's upscale district. This designer store showcases a curated selection of high-end fashion brands, catering to aficionados of luxury apparel, accessories, and footwear. From the iconic red soles of Christian Louboutin to the timeless elegance of Givenchy and Saint Laurent, La Maison du Luxe offers a coveted collection of designer pieces. Prices at this boutique reflect the exclusivity of the brands, with dresses ranging from €1000 to €5000 and shoes starting at €700. La Maison du Luxe welcomes shoppers from 10:30 AM to 7:30 PM, allowing ample time for indulging in luxury retail therapy. Accessing this designer haven is convenient, as it lies within walking distance from the city center or can be reached via tram, with the Grand Théâtre stop being the closest.

Bordeaux Couture: Where Style Meets Artistry

Situated in the eclectic Quartier des Chartrons, Bordeaux Couture celebrates the marriage of style and artistry with its curated collection of designer fashion and accessories. This boutique prides itself on showcasing emerging designers alongside established fashion houses, offering a diverse range of styles to suit every taste. From avant-garde creations to classic silhouettes, Bordeaux Couture caters to fashion enthusiasts seeking unique and innovative designs. Prices at this boutique vary depending on the designer and collection, with dresses ranging from €200 to €1500 and accessories starting at €50. Bordeaux Couture opens its doors from 11:00 AM to 7:00 PM, providing ample opportunity for a leisurely shopping experience. Accessing this boutique is convenient, as it is located near tram stops at Chartrons or Cours du Médoc, allowing visitors to explore the charming neighborhood before or after their shopping excursion.

Rive Gauche Boutique: Bohemian Chic in Bordeaux

Embracing Bordeaux's bohemian spirit, Rive Gauche Boutique offers a curated selection of eclectic fashion and accessories that celebrate individuality and creativity. Situated on the left bank of the Garonne River, this boutique exudes laid-back charm with its cozy interior and eclectic decor. Visitors can peruse a diverse range of clothing, jewelry, and home goods, each imbued with a sense of bohemian chic. From flowy maxi dresses to artisanal jewelry and handcrafted textiles, Rive Gauche Boutique caters to free-spirited souls seeking unique and expressive pieces. Prices at this boutique are reasonable, with dresses ranging from €50 to €300 and accessories starting at €20. Rive Gauche Boutique welcomes shoppers from 11:00 AM to 6:00 PM, providing ample time to explore its treasure trove of bohemian delights. Accessing this boutique is convenient, as it is located near tram stops at Place du Palais or can be reached by a leisurely stroll from the city center, allowing visitors to soak in the artistic ambiance of the left bank.

La Boutique Vintage: Timeless Treasures and Retro Finds

For lovers of vintage fashion and retro charm, La Boutique Vintage offers a nostalgic journey through decades past with its curated collection of clothing, accessories, and decor. Tucked away in the quaint streets of Bordeaux's historic center, this boutique transports visitors to a bygone era with its carefully curated selection of vintage finds. From classic denim and leather jackets to statement accessories and mid-century furniture, La Boutique Vintage caters to vintage enthusiasts seeking unique and timeless pieces. Prices at this boutique vary depending on the rarity and condition of the items, with clothing ranging from €20 to €200 and furniture starting at €50. La Boutique Vintage opens its doors from 10:00 AM to 7:00 PM, providing ample time for a nostalgic shopping experience. Accessing this boutique is convenient, as it is situated near tram stops at Place de la Bourse or can be reached by a leisurely stroll from the city center, allowing visitors to explore Bordeaux's historic streets and landmarks along the way.

Bordeaux's boutiques and designer stores offer a diverse array of shopping experiences, each catering to unique tastes and preferences. Whether indulging in luxury fashion, exploring emerging designers, or uncovering vintage treasures, visitors are sure to find their perfect shopping destination amidst Bordeaux's charming streets and neighborhoods. With convenient access via tram and a plethora of options to suit every budget and style, embarking on a shopping adventure in Bordeaux is an unforgettable experience that promises to delight and inspire.

9.3 Antique Markets and Flea Markets

In Bordeaux, the allure of antiquity beckons visitors to explore the city's charming antique markets and flea markets, where hidden treasures await discovery amidst the hustle and bustle of vibrant stalls and eclectic vendors. Embarking on a journey through these markets offers a glimpse into Bordeaux's rich history and cultural heritage, with each venue boasting its unique atmosphere and selection of goods.

Marché aux Puces de Saint-Michel: A Treasure Trove of Vintage Finds

Nestled in the heart of Bordeaux's historic Saint-Michel district, the Marché aux Puces de Saint-Michel stands as a testament to the city's enduring love affair with all things vintage and eclectic. This sprawling flea market, held every Sunday along the quays of the Garonne River, offers a treasure trove of antique furniture, retro clothing, vintage accessories, and quirky collectibles. Visitors can meander through the labyrinth of stalls, browsing an eclectic mix of goods ranging from mid-century modern gems to nostalgic memorabilia. Prices at the Marché aux Puces de Saint-Michel vary depending on the rarity and condition of the items, with bargains to be found for those with a keen eye for vintage charm. The market typically opens in the early morning, around 7:00 AM, and winds down by mid-afternoon. Accessing the Marché aux Puces de Saint-Michel is convenient, as it is located within walking distance from the city center or accessible via tram, with stops at Saint-Michel or Place de la Bourse.

Marché des Quais: Riverside Rendezvous for Antiques

Perched along the picturesque Quai des Chartrons, the Marché des Quais enchants visitors with its scenic setting and eclectic array of antiques and vintage wares. Held on selected weekends from spring to autumn, this riverside market transforms the quays into a bustling hub of activity, attracting vendors and collectors from near and far. Here, visitors can peruse a diverse selection of goods, including antique furniture, retro decor, vintage clothing, and artisanal crafts. The ambiance is lively, with live music and food stalls adding to the festive atmosphere. Prices at the Marché des Quais vary depending on the vendor and the uniqueness of the items, with opportunities to haggle for a bargain. The market typically operates from 9:00 AM to 6:00 PM on Saturdays and Sundays during the market season. Accessing the Marché des Quais is straightforward, as it is situated along the riverfront and easily reachable by tram, with stops at Chartrons or Quinconces.

Brocante de la Place Saint-Michel: A Quaint Neighborhood Market
Tucked away in the charming Place Saint-Michel, the Brocante de la Place Saint-Michel offers a quaint and intimate setting for antique enthusiasts to explore. Held on selected weekends throughout the year, this neighborhood market exudes a relaxed ambiance, with vendors setting up stalls beneath the shadow of the iconic Saint-Michel Basilica. Visitors can browse a curated selection of antiques, vintage goods, and bric-a-brac, ranging from old books and vinyl records to antique kitchenware and retro toys. Prices at the Brocante de la Place Saint-Michel are reasonable, with opportunities to uncover unique finds at affordable prices. The market typically opens in the late morning and concludes by early evening, allowing visitors to leisurely explore the stalls at their own pace. Accessing the Brocante de la Place Saint-Michel is convenient, as it is located within walking distance from the city center and accessible by tram, with stops at Saint-Michel or Place de la Victoire.

Marché du Livre Ancien et d'Occasion: A Literary Treasure Trove

For book lovers and bibliophiles, the Marché du Livre Ancien et d'Occasion offers a literary treasure trove amidst Bordeaux's bustling city center. Held every Saturday along the Allées de Tourny, this open-air book market boasts a vast selection of antique books, rare manuscripts, and vintage prints. Visitors can peruse the stalls of local book dealers and collectors, uncovering literary gems spanning genres and eras. From classic novels and poetry collections to historical tomes and art books, the Marché du Livre Ancien et d'Occasion caters to book enthusiasts of all interests. Prices for books at the market vary depending on their rarity, condition, and age, with options available to suit every budget. The market typically operates from 9:00 AM to 6:00 PM, allowing ample time for browsing and literary exploration. Accessing the Marché du Livre Ancien et d'Occasion is convenient, as it is situated in the city center and easily reachable by tram, with stops at Quinconces or Grand Théâtre.

Marché de la Brocante Place du Parlement: Timeless Charm in Historic Surroundings

Nestled amidst the grandeur of Bordeaux's historic center, the Marché de la Brocante Place du Parlement offers a glimpse into the city's storied past with its charming array of antiques and vintage treasures. Held on selected weekends throughout the year in the shadow of the imposing Palais de la Bourse, this atmospheric market beckons visitors to wander through its stalls in search of hidden gems. Here, antique aficionados can unearth a diverse selection of goods, including antique furniture, vintage textiles, retro homeware, and quirky curiosities. Prices at the Marché de la Brocante Place du Parlement vary depending on the vendor and the uniqueness of the items, with opportunities to discover affordable finds alongside higher-end collectibles. The market typically opens in the late morning and concludes by early evening, providing ample time for leisurely browsing. Accessing the Marché de la Brocante Place du Parlement is convenient, as it is located in the city center and easily reachable by tram, with stops at Place de la Bourse or Quinconces.

Bordeaux's antique markets and flea markets offer a delightful blend of history, culture, and discovery, providing visitors with an opportunity to uncover hidden treasures and immerse themselves in the city's vibrant atmosphere. From riverside rendezvous to quaint neighborhood markets, each venue boasts its unique charm and selection of goods, inviting visitors to embark on a journey of exploration and nostalgia. With convenient access via tram and a plethora of options to suit every taste and budget, a visit to Bordeaux's antique markets is an unforgettable experience that promises to delight and inspire.

9.4 Souvenirs and Gifts

In Bordeaux, the quest for the perfect souvenir or gift is a delightful journey through the city's charming streets and eclectic shops, where a plethora of unique treasures awaits discovery. From quaint boutiques nestled in historic neighborhoods to bustling markets teeming with local crafts, Bordeaux offers a diverse array of options for souvenir and gift shopping, each venue showcasing the city's rich culture and heritage.

La Cité du Vin Boutique: Celebrating Bordeaux's Wine Culture

Perched on the banks of the Garonne River, La Cité du Vin stands as a symbol of Bordeaux's illustrious wine culture, offering visitors an immersive journey through the world of oenology. Within its walls lies the La Cité du Vin Boutique, a treasure trove of wine-related souvenirs and gifts. Here, visitors can peruse a curated selection of Bordeaux wines, wine accessories, books, and gourmet treats, each celebrating the region's vinous heritage. Prices at the boutique vary depending on the items, with options to suit every budget, from affordable trinkets to exclusive wine collections. The boutique typically opens from 10:00 AM to 7:00 PM, with extended hours during peak tourist seasons. Accessing La Cité du Vin Boutique is convenient, as it is located near the city center and easily reachable by tram, with stops at Bassins à Flot or La Cité du Vin.

Marché des Capucins: Gastronomic Delights and Local Crafts

Nestled in Bordeaux's vibrant Capucins district, the Marché des Capucins beckons visitors with its bustling atmosphere and diverse array of stalls. While primarily known for its fresh produce and gourmet delights, the market also boasts a selection of souvenir and gift shops offering local crafts and artisanal products. Visitors can browse through stalls selling handmade ceramics, regional delicacies, and unique souvenirs inspired by Bordeaux's culinary and cultural heritage. Prices at the Marché des Capucins vary depending on the items, with options available to suit every budget, from affordable trinkets to artisanal masterpieces. The market typically operates from early morning until mid-afternoon, providing ample time for souvenir shopping amidst the lively ambiance.

Accessing the Marché des Capucins is convenient, as it is located near the city center and easily reachable by tram, with stops at Capucins or Saint-Michel.

Maison du Tourisme Boutique: Bordeaux-Inspired Gifts and Memorabilia

Located in the heart of Bordeaux's historic center, the Maison du Tourisme Boutique invites visitors to discover a curated selection of Bordeaux-inspired gifts and memorabilia. Here, visitors can find an array of souvenirs celebrating the city's landmarks, heritage, and culture, including postcards, posters, and locally crafted keepsakes. Additionally, the boutique offers a selection of Bordeaux wines and gourmet products, allowing visitors to take a taste of the city home with them. Prices at the Maison du Tourisme Boutique vary depending on the items, with options available to suit every budget, from inexpensive mementos to exclusive gifts. The boutique typically opens from 10:00 AM to 6:00 PM, providing ample time for souvenir shopping during a day of exploration. Accessing the Maison du Tourisme Boutique is convenient, as it is situated in the city center and easily reachable on foot or by tram, with stops at Gambetta or Grand Théâtre.

Rue Sainte-Catherine Boutiques: Fashionable Finds and Bordeaux-Inspired Gifts

Stretching over 1.2 kilometers, Rue Sainte-Catherine stands as one of Europe's longest shopping streets, offering visitors a plethora of boutiques and shops to explore. Among the fashion boutiques and international brands, visitors can also find a selection of shops offering

Bordeaux-inspired gifts and souvenirs. From stylish Bordeaux-themed apparel to locally made crafts and accessories, these boutiques cater to visitors seeking unique mementos of their time in the city. Prices at the Rue Sainte-Catherine boutiques vary depending on the items, with options available to suit every budget, from budget-friendly trinkets to luxury souvenirs. The boutiques typically open from 10:00 AM to 8:00 PM, providing ample time for souvenir shopping amidst the bustling street scene. Accessing Rue Sainte-Catherine is convenient, as it is located in the city center and easily reachable on foot or by tram, with stops at Place de la Comédie or Quinconces.

Quartier des Chartrons: Artisanal Crafts and Vintage Finds

In the picturesque Quartier des Chartrons, visitors can explore a treasure trove of boutiques and shops offering artisanal crafts and vintage finds. This historic neighborhood, once the epicenter of Bordeaux's wine trade, now boasts a vibrant arts and culture scene, with boutiques showcasing locally made products and unique souvenirs. Visitors can browse through shops selling handmade jewelry, ceramics, artwork, and vintage treasures, each reflecting the neighborhood's creative spirit and heritage. Prices in the Quartier des Chartrons vary depending on the items, with options available to suit every budget, from affordable crafts to high-end collectibles. The boutiques typically open from late morning until early evening, providing ample time for leisurely exploration. Accessing the Quartier des Chartrons is convenient, as it is located near the city center and easily reachable on foot or by tram, with stops at Chartrons or Cours du Médoc.

Bordeaux's souvenir and gift shopping scene offer a diverse array of options for visitors seeking unique mementos of their time in the city. From wine-themed gifts to locally crafted souvenirs and vintage treasures, each venue provides an opportunity to discover the rich culture and heritage of Bordeaux. With convenient access via tram and a plethora of options to suit every taste and budget, souvenir shopping in Bordeaux is an enjoyable and memorable experience that promises to delight and inspire visitors.

9.5 Specialty Stores: Wine, Cheese, and Gourmet Products

In Bordeaux, culinary aficionados are spoiled for choice with an abundance of specialty stores offering a tantalizing array of gourmet delights. From world-renowned wines to artisanal cheeses and gourmet delicacies, these specialty stores promise a sensory journey through the flavors of Bordeaux and beyond.

La Vinothèque: A Wine Lover's Paradise

Nestled in the heart of Bordeaux's historic center, La Vinothèque stands as a mecca for wine enthusiasts seeking to explore the region's rich viticultural heritage. This specialty wine store boasts an extensive selection of Bordeaux wines, ranging from prestigious Grand Crus to hidden gems from lesser-known appellations. Visitors can peruse the shelves lined with bottles of reds, whites, and rosés, each carefully curated to showcase the diversity and quality of Bordeaux's winemaking traditions. Prices at La Vinothèque vary depending on the vintage, producer, and rarity of the wines, with options available to suit every budget, from affordable everyday sippers to investment-worthy collectibles. The store typically opens from 10:00 AM to 7:00 PM, providing ample time for wine tasting and exploration. Accessing La Vinothèque is convenient, as it is located near the city center and easily reachable on foot or by tram, with stops at Gambetta or Grand Théâtre.

Fromagerie Deruelle: A Haven for Cheese Connoisseurs

For lovers of fromage, Fromagerie Deruelle offers a veritable treasure trove of artisanal cheeses sourced from across France and beyond. Located in Bordeaux's bustling Capucins district, this specialty cheese shop showcases an extensive selection of cheeses, from creamy Camemberts to tangy Roqueforts and everything in between. Visitors can sample and purchase cheeses by the wedge or opt for pre-selected cheese boards curated by the knowledgeable staff. Prices at Fromagerie Deruelle vary depending on the type and origin of the cheese, with options available to suit every palate and budget. The shop typically opens from early morning until mid-afternoon, providing ample time for cheese tasting and exploration. Accessing Fromagerie Deruelle is convenient, as it is situated near the city center and easily reachable by tram, with stops at Capucins or Saint-Michel.

Epicerie Fine L'Intendant: Gourmet Delicacies in a Historic Setting

Housed in a beautifully restored 18th-century building in Bordeaux's Golden Triangle, Epicerie Fine L'Intendant offers a luxurious shopping experience for discerning gourmands. This specialty gourmet store showcases an exquisite selection of delicacies, including foie gras, truffles, caviar, and other gourmet treats sourced from top producers around the world. Visitors can browse through the impeccably curated shelves, indulging in the finest culinary delights and gourmet ingredients. Prices at Epicerie Fine L'Intendant reflect the premium quality and exclusivity of the products, with options available to suit every taste and occasion. The store typically opens from 10:00 AM to 7:00 PM, providing ample time for culinary exploration and indulgence. Accessing Epicerie Fine L'Intendant is convenient, as it is located in the city center and easily reachable on foot or by tram, with stops at Grand Théâtre or Quinconces.

La Chocolaterie de Bordeaux: Sweet Temptations and Artisanal Chocolates

Indulge in the sweet pleasures of chocolate at La Chocolaterie de Bordeaux, a boutique chocolatier specializing in handcrafted chocolates and confections. Located in the picturesque Quartier des Chartrons, this specialty chocolate shop offers a delectable selection of truffles, pralines, and chocolate bars made with the finest ingredients and traditional techniques. Visitors can delight in the rich aromas and flavors of Belgian, Swiss, and French chocolates, each meticulously crafted to perfection. Prices at La Chocolaterie de Bordeaux vary depending on the type and quantity of chocolates, with options available to suit every craving and budget. The shop typically opens from late morning until early evening, providing ample time for chocolate tasting and indulgence. Accessing La Chocolaterie de Bordeaux is convenient, as it is located near the city center and easily reachable by tram, with stops at Chartrons or Cours du Médoc.

La Maison du Thé: A Tea Lover's Sanctuary

Escape the hustle and bustle of the city and embark on a sensory journey through the world of tea at La Maison du Thé. Situated in Bordeaux's charming Saint-Pierre district, this specialty tea shop offers a curated selection of fine teas sourced from renowned tea estates around the globe. Visitors can explore a diverse range of flavors and blends, from delicate green teas to robust black teas and aromatic herbal infusions. Prices at La Maison du Thé vary depending on the type and origin of the teas, with options available to suit every palate and preference. The shop typically opens from 10:00 AM to 7:00 PM, providing ample time for tea tasting and relaxation. Accessing La Maison du Thé is convenient, as it is located near the city center and easily reachable on foot or by tram, with stops at Saint-Pierre or Place de la Bourse.

Bordeaux's specialty stores offer a culinary playground for food and drink enthusiasts, showcasing the region's rich gastronomic heritage and global influences. Whether indulging in Bordeaux wines, artisanal cheeses, gourmet delicacies, or sweet treats, visitors are sure to find their perfect culinary treasure amidst the city's vibrant streets and historic neighborhoods. With convenient access via tram and a plethora of options to suit every taste and budget, specialty shopping in Bordeaux is an unforgettable experience that promises to delight and inspire the senses.

CHAPTER 10

DAY TRIPS AND EXCURSIONS

10.1 Wine Tours to Bordeaux's Vineyards

Embarking on a journey to the renowned Bordeaux vineyards is not just a trip; it's an immersive experience into the heart of French winemaking culture. Each vineyard offers a unique blend of history, tradition, and innovation, making it a captivating destination for wine enthusiasts and curious travelers alike.

Exploring Médoc: Unveiling Bordeaux's Legacy

Médoc, situated on the left bank of the Gironde estuary, boasts a prestigious reputation for producing some of Bordeaux's most celebrated wines. As you traverse through the picturesque countryside, you'll encounter sprawling vineyards adorned with meticulously tended vines, casting a mesmerizing vista. Visitors can anticipate guided tours through esteemed châteaux like Château Margaux and Château Lafite Rothschild, where they'll delve into centuries-old winemaking techniques and savor exquisite tastings of the region's famed red blends, notably Cabernet Sauvignon and Merlot.

Saint-Émilion: A Journey into Timeless Elegance

Nestled on Bordeaux's right bank, Saint-Émilion exudes a charming ambiance, characterized by its cobbled streets, medieval architecture, and limestone cliffs. Here, amidst the quaint village setting, visitors are treated to an enchanting exploration of historic vineyards such as Château Ausone and Château Cheval Blanc. Expect immersive cellar tours, where the secrets of Saint-Émilion's esteemed Grand Cru Classé wines are unveiled. Indulge in tastings of velvety Merlots and robust Cabernet Francs, all while soaking in the region's rich cultural heritage.

Pomerol: Discovering Hidden Gems

Pomerol, though smaller in size compared to its neighboring regions, holds an esteemed status in Bordeaux's winemaking landscape. This intimate terroir is renowned for producing exceptional Merlot-dominant wines, celebrated for their opulence and finesse. Visitors embarking on a wine tour of Pomerol can anticipate intimate tastings at renowned estates like Pétrus and Château La Fleur-Pétrus, where they'll witness firsthand the meticulous craftsmanship behind each bottle. Prepare to be captivated by Pomerol's rustic charm and the unparalleled quality of its illustrious vintages.

Graves and Sauternes: A Symphony of Terroirs

The Graves and Sauternes regions, nestled south of Bordeaux, offer a contrasting yet equally captivating wine experience. Here, amidst rolling vine-covered hills and verdant landscapes, visitors can explore a diverse array of terroirs, from gravelly soils ideal for producing robust reds to limestone-rich terrain conducive to crafting exquisite sweet wines. Delve into the storied cellars of esteemed estates such as Château Haut-Brion and Château d'Yquem, where age-old traditions intertwine with modern winemaking innovations. Sample the full spectrum of Bordeaux's offerings, from bold, tannic reds to lusciously sweet dessert wines, all while savoring the region's breathtaking scenery.

Entre-Deux-Mers: A Haven of Hidden Treasures

Situated between the Garonne and Dordogne rivers, Entre-Deux-Mers embodies Bordeaux's bucolic charm and agricultural heritage. This lesser-known region is a haven for discovery, boasting a diverse range of vineyards, châteaux, and family-owned wineries. Visitors can embark on leisurely wine tours, meandering through sun-drenched vineyards and sampling a myriad of varietals, from crisp Sauvignon Blancs to aromatic Semillons. Embrace the warm hospitality of local winemakers as they share their passion for winemaking and offer insights into the region's distinctive terroir.

A day trip or excursion to Bordeaux's vineyards promises an unforgettable journey through the heart of French winemaking tradition. Whether exploring the esteemed appellations of Médoc and Saint-Émilion or uncovering hidden gems in Pomerol and

Entre-Deux-Mers, visitors are invited to immerse themselves in a tapestry of wine and culture. From centuries-old châteaux to quaint family estates, each vineyard offers a unique glimpse into Bordeaux's rich winemaking heritage, leaving indelible memories and a newfound appreciation for the artistry behind every bottle.

10.2 Coastal Escapes: Arcachon and Cap Ferret

Embarking on a day trip or excursion from Bordeaux to its coastal escapes offers travelers a delightful blend of natural beauty, seaside charm, and culinary delights. From the tranquil shores of Arcachon to the rugged landscapes of Cap Ferret, each destination promises an unforgettable experience that beckons visitors to unwind and explore.

Arcachon: A Seaside Haven of Tranquility

Nestled along the shimmering waters of the Atlantic Ocean, Arcachon beckons with its pristine beaches, azure seas, and vibrant waterfront promenade. A day trip to Arcachon unveils a myriad of activities, from leisurely strolls along the bustling marina to exhilarating water sports adventures. Visitors can ascend the iconic Dune du Pilat, Europe's tallest sand dune, to marvel at panoramic views of the coastline or indulge in freshly shucked oysters at one of the local oyster farms. Don't miss the opportunity to cruise around the tranquil waters of the Arcachon Bay aboard a traditional pinasse boat, soaking in the beauty of the surrounding landscapes.

Cap Ferret: Exploring Untamed Beauty

For those seeking a more rugged coastal escape, Cap Ferret offers a pristine sanctuary of untamed beauty and natural wonder. Situated at the tip of a narrow peninsula, Cap Ferret boasts windswept beaches, dense pine forests, and sweeping vistas of the Atlantic Ocean and the Arcachon Bay. Visitors can embark on scenic hikes through the Cap Ferret Lighthouse Reserve, where verdant trails lead to panoramic viewpoints overlooking the coastline. Alternatively, unwind on secluded stretches of sandy shores, where the rhythmic crash of waves provides a soothing soundtrack to the day. Indulge in freshly caught seafood at one of Cap Ferret's charming waterfront eateries, savoring the flavors of the sea amidst breathtaking surroundings.

Bassin d'Arcachon: A Paradise for Nature Enthusiasts

The Bassin d'Arcachon, a tranquil lagoon nestled between the mainland and the Atlantic coast, beckons nature enthusiasts with its diverse ecosystems and abundant wildlife. A day excursion to this coastal gem offers opportunities for birdwatching, kayaking, and exploring pristine nature reserves. Join a guided boat tour to discover the hidden treasures of the Bassin, from picturesque fishing villages to secluded bird sanctuaries teeming with avian life. Be sure to sample local delicacies such as Arcachon Bay's famed seafood platters, featuring succulent oysters, mussels, and shrimp harvested fresh from the surrounding waters.

Cap Ferret Peninsula: A Playground for Outdoor Enthusiasts

The Cap Ferret Peninsula is a playground for outdoor enthusiasts, boasting a wealth of recreational activities amidst breathtaking natural landscapes. Visitors can embark on scenic cycling tours along the peninsula's network of bike paths, winding through pine forests, dune landscapes, and quaint fishing villages. Take to the waters for a day of sailing, windsurfing, or paddleboarding, or simply relax on sun-drenched beaches, basking in the serenity of this coastal paradise. Don't forget to explore the charming town of Cap Ferret, where colorful boutiques, bustling markets, and seafood shacks await discovery.

Day trips and excursions to Bordeaux's coastal escapes offer travelers a perfect blend of adventure and serenity amidst stunning natural landscapes. Whether exploring the pristine shores of Arcachon, the rugged beauty of Cap Ferret, or the tranquil waters of the Bassin d'Arcachon, visitors are invited to immerse themselves in the coastal charm and laid-back lifestyle of this enchanting region. With an array of activities, attractions, and culinary delights to discover, a day trip from Bordeaux to its coastal escapes promises an unforgettable experience that will leave lasting memories for years to come.

10.3 Medieval Towns and Historic Villages

Embarking on day trips and excursions from Bordeaux to explore medieval towns and historic villages is like stepping back in time to an era of knights, cobblestone streets, and ancient fortifications. These charming destinations, nestled amidst picturesque landscapes, offer visitors a glimpse into centuries of rich history, cultural heritage, and architectural marvels.

Saint-Émilion: A Timeless Treasure

Saint-Émilion, a UNESCO World Heritage Site, beckons travelers with its timeless charm and rich winemaking heritage. Nestled amidst rolling vineyards and lush countryside, this medieval town exudes an air of romanticism, with its cobbled streets, ancient stone buildings, and towering spires. Visitors can wander through winding alleyways lined with artisanal shops, wine cellars, and quaint cafés, soaking in the ambiance of this historic enclave. Don't miss the opportunity to explore the underground catacombs and monolithic church carved into the limestone cliffs, offering a fascinating glimpse into Saint-Émilion's storied past.

Sarlat-la-Canéda: A Journey Through Medieval Splendor

Nestled in the heart of the Dordogne region, Sarlat-la-Canéda enchants visitors with its exceptionally well-preserved medieval architecture and bustling market squares. As you meander through the town's labyrinthine streets, you'll encounter an array of historic landmarks, including the imposing Sarlat Cathedral, the fortified Church of Sainte-Marie, and the elegant Renaissance mansions adorned with intricately carved facades. Immerse yourself in the vibrant atmosphere of the weekly market, where the scents of fresh produce, local delicacies, and artisan crafts mingle enticingly. Sarlat's timeless beauty and cultural richness make it a must-visit destination for history enthusiasts and avid explorers alike.

Rocamadour: A Pilgrimage to Spiritual Splendor

Perched dramatically atop a sheer limestone cliff overlooking the Alzou Valley, Rocamadour is a pilgrimage site of unparalleled beauty and spiritual significance. This medieval village, with its tiered buildings clinging precariously to the rocky precipice, has been a place of worship and devotion for centuries. Visitors can ascend the Grand Escalier, a monumental staircase flanked by ancient chapels and shrines, to reach the revered Sanctuary of the Blessed Virgin Mary. Marvel at the breathtaking views from the Belvedere des Hospitaux, where the surrounding landscape stretches out in a panorama of rugged beauty. Whether exploring the sacred sites or wandering through the charming streets lined with artisan shops and cafés, Rocamadour offers a transcendent experience that resonates with history and reverence.

La Rochelle: A Maritime Jewel

Situated along the sun-drenched shores of the Bay of Biscay, La Rochelle beckons visitors with its maritime heritage, historic harbor, and vibrant waterfront promenade. This bustling port city boasts a wealth of architectural treasures, from the imposing towers of the medieval Old Port to the elegant arcades of the Place de Verdun. Explore the atmospheric streets of the Vieux Port district, where ancient ramparts and fortified gates hint at the city's storied past. Discover the maritime history of La Rochelle at the Museum of the New World, housed within a beautifully restored 18th-century mansion, or embark on a boat excursion to the nearby Île de Ré, renowned for its pristine beaches and charming villages. With its blend of history, culture, and coastal beauty, La

Rochelle offers a captivating escape for travelers seeking to immerse themselves in the romance of the past.

Day trips and excursions from Bordeaux to medieval towns and historic villages promise a journey through time, where each destination offers a unique tapestry of history, architecture, and cultural heritage. Whether exploring the timeless streets of Saint-Émilion, the medieval splendor of Sarlat-la-Canéda, the spiritual allure of Rocamadour, or the maritime charm of La Rochelle, visitors are invited to delve into centuries of rich history and immerse themselves in the enchanting ambiance of these storied locales. With their captivating beauty and timeless appeal, these coastal escapes offer an unforgettable experience that will linger in the hearts and minds of travelers long after they've returned home.

10.4 Cognac and the Charente Region

Embarking on day trips and excursions from Bordeaux to the coastal escapes of Cognac and the Charente Region unveils a journey of discovery through rolling vineyards, historic towns, and scenic waterways. These enchanting destinations, steeped in tradition and renowned for their world-class spirits, offer visitors a captivating blend of cultural heritage, natural beauty, and gastronomic delights.

Cognac: A Spirit of Heritage

Nestled along the tranquil banks of the Charente River, the town of Cognac beckons travelers with its storied history and legendary eaux-de-vie. A day trip to Cognac promises a fascinating exploration of centuries-old distilleries, where visitors can witness the intricate process of crafting this iconic spirit. Embark on guided tours of renowned cognac houses such as Rémy Martin, Hennessy, and Martell, where master blenders share their expertise and unveil the secrets behind the art of aging and blending. Delve into the town's rich heritage at the Cognac Museum, housed within the elegant confines of the Château des Valois, and stroll along the picturesque Quai de la Charente, lined with historic warehouses and bustling cafés. Don't miss the opportunity to sample a variety of cognacs during guided tastings, savoring the nuanced flavors and aromas of this beloved French libation.

Jarnac: A Riverside Retreat

Located just a short distance from Cognac, the charming town of Jarnac offers a tranquil riverside retreat amidst verdant vineyards and historic landmarks. Visitors can explore the birthplace of former French President François Mitterrand at the Maison de la Lieutenance, a beautifully preserved 16th-century mansion overlooking the Charente River. Wander through the town's picturesque streets, lined with half-timbered houses, quaint boutiques, and inviting bistros. Embark on leisurely boat cruises along the scenic waterways, admiring the idyllic landscapes and lush greenery that characterize the Charente region. Whether sampling local delicacies at traditional brasseries or simply soaking in the serene ambiance of this riverside gem, Jarnac offers a peaceful escape from the hustle and bustle of city life.

Angoulême: A City of Art and Culture

Perched atop a rocky promontory overlooking the Charente River, the city of Angoulême captivates visitors with its rich artistic heritage and medieval charm. Explore the city's historic center, where ancient ramparts, majestic cathedrals, and winding cobblestone streets offer a glimpse into its illustrious past. Art enthusiasts will delight in the vibrant street art scene that has earned Angoulême the title of "Capital of Comics," with colorful murals adorning buildings throughout the city. Discover the works of renowned artists at the Musée d'Angoulême, housed within a former Benedictine abbey, or stroll along the Promenade des Remparts for panoramic views of the surrounding countryside. With its dynamic cultural scene, eclectic dining options, and scenic vistas, Angoulême promises a memorable day trip for visitors seeking to immerse themselves in the artistry and history of the Charente region.

Cognac Vineyards: A Terroir of Distinction
Beyond the historic towns and bustling cities, the rolling vineyards of the Cognac region offer visitors a glimpse into the terroir of distinction that produces the world's finest eaux-de-vie. Embark on guided tours of family-owned estates and boutique wineries, where generations of winemakers have cultivated the grapes that form the foundation of Cognac's renowned spirits. Learn about the region's unique soils, microclimates, and grape varietals as you meander through sun-drenched vineyards and verdant landscapes. Indulge in tastings of aged cognacs and pineau des Charentes, a delightful apéritif made from a blend of grape must and Cognac, while soaking in the breathtaking vistas of the surrounding countryside. Whether exploring the historic towns or wandering through the scenic vineyards, a day trip to the Cognac region offers a captivating journey through the essence of French artisanship and tradition.

Day trips and excursions from Bordeaux to Cognac and the Charente region offer visitors a voyage of discovery through centuries of history, tradition, and natural beauty. Whether exploring the storied streets of Cognac, the tranquil riverside retreats of Jarnac and Angoulême, or the scenic vineyards that dot the countryside, travelers are invited to immerse themselves in the essence of French craftsmanship and hospitality. With its rich cultural heritage, gastronomic delights, and picturesque landscapes, the coastal escapes of Cognac and the Charente region promise an unforgettable experience that will linger in the hearts and minds of visitors long after they've returned home.

10.5 Pyrenees Mountains and Basque Country

Embarking on day trips and excursions from Bordeaux to the Pyrenees Mountains and Basque Country offers travelers a harmonious fusion of breathtaking landscapes, rich cultural heritage, and culinary delights. These diverse destinations, nestled between rugged coastlines and majestic peaks, invite visitors to immerse themselves in the beauty and vibrancy of southwestern France.

Biarritz: A Coastal Gem

Perched along the Bay of Biscay, the coastal town of Biarritz beckons with its sandy beaches, rugged cliffs, and vibrant surf culture. A day trip to Biarritz promises sun-drenched days spent lounging on golden shores, surfing the waves, or exploring the town's charming streets lined with elegant Belle Époque villas and trendy boutiques. Don't miss the chance to witness the powerful spectacle of waves crashing against the iconic Rocher de la Vierge, a rocky outcrop crowned by a statue of the Virgin

Mary, or indulge in freshly caught seafood at one of the local seaside cafés. With its laid-back atmosphere and stunning coastal vistas, Biarritz offers a perfect escape for beach lovers and outdoor enthusiasts alike.

Saint-Jean-de-Luz: A Seaside Sanctuary

Nestled along the Basque coast, Saint-Jean-de-Luz enchants visitors with its picturesque harbor, colorful fishermen's cottages, and lively waterfront promenade. Explore the town's historic center, where narrow cobblestone streets lead to quaint squares and centuries-old churches, or wander along the bustling quayside, where fishermen unload their daily catch. Relax on the sandy shores of the Grande Plage, framed by towering cliffs and swaying palm trees, or venture out to the rugged coastline to discover hidden coves and secluded beaches. Saint-Jean-de-Luz's unique blend of Basque tradition and coastal charm makes it a captivating destination for travelers seeking tranquility and natural beauty.

Hendaye: Where Mountains Meet the Sea

Situated at the border between France and Spain, Hendaye offers a scenic blend of mountainous landscapes and sandy beaches, making it an ideal destination for outdoor adventures and seaside relaxation. Spend the day hiking through lush green valleys and pine forests in the foothills of the Pyrenees, or bask in the sun on Hendaye's expansive beach, where gentle waves lap against the shore. Explore the town's historic quarter, with its traditional Basque architecture and lively markets, or embark on a boat excursion along the coast to discover hidden coves and marine wildlife. With its pristine natural surroundings and laid-back ambiance, Hendaye offers a tranquil retreat for visitors seeking to escape the hustle and bustle of city life.

Biarritz to Bayonne: A Journey Through Basque Culture

Embark on a scenic drive from Biarritz to the historic city of Bayonne, where centuries-old traditions and Basque culture come to life amidst charming medieval streets and picturesque riverbanks. Explore Bayonne's historic center, where Gothic cathedrals, Renaissance palaces, and fortified ramparts bear witness to the city's storied past. Stroll along the banks of the Adour River, lined with colorful half-timbered houses and bustling cafés, or sample traditional Basque cuisine at one of the local bistros, where savory pintxos and hearty stews reign supreme. Don't miss the chance to visit the Musée Basque, housed within a former 17th-century convent, to learn about the region's rich cultural heritage and artistic traditions. With its blend of history, culture, and gastronomy, Bayonne offers a captivating glimpse into the heart of Basque Country.

Pyrenees Mountains: A Playground for Outdoor Enthusiasts

Beyond the coastal towns and charming villages, the Pyrenees Mountains beckon adventurers with their rugged peaks, pristine lakes, and alpine meadows. Embark on guided hikes through breathtaking landscapes, where cascading waterfalls, towering cliffs, and panoramic vistas await around every bend. Explore quaint mountain villages like Saint-Jean-Pied-de-Port and Laruns, where stone cottages and ancient churches provide a glimpse into rural life in the Pyrenees. For thrill-seekers, the mountains offer a wealth of outdoor activities, from skiing and snowboarding in the winter to rock climbing and paragliding in the summer. With its untamed beauty and boundless opportunities for exploration, the Pyrenees Mountains offer a playground for outdoor enthusiasts and nature lovers alike.

Day trips and excursions from Bordeaux to the Pyrenees Mountains and Basque Country promise a captivating journey through a tapestry of nature and culture. Whether exploring the coastal towns of Biarritz, Saint-Jean-de-Luz, and Hendaye, or venturing into the mountainous landscapes of the Pyrenees, visitors are invited to immerse themselves in the beauty, history, and traditions of southwestern France. With its stunning vistas, vibrant communities, and diverse range of activities, this coastal region offers an unforgettable experience that will leave lasting memories for years to come.

CHAPTER 11

ENTERTAINMENT AND NIGHTLIFE

11.1 Live Music Venues and Concert Halls

Welcome to Bordeaux, where the melody of life resonates in every corner, echoing through its streets, cafes, and concert halls. As a veteran traveler and author, I've traversed the globe seeking out the most enchanting live music venues, and Bordeaux has never failed to captivate me with its harmonious offerings. In this guide, I invite you to join me on a lyrical journey through five of Bordeaux's most vibrant and soul-stirring concert halls and live music venues.

Le Rocher de Palmer: Where Music Meets Diversity

Nestled on the right bank of the Garonne River, Le Rocher de Palmer stands as a beacon of musical diversity in Bordeaux. This dynamic venue hosts an eclectic array of performances, ranging from jazz and blues to world music and electronic beats. Step inside its industrial-chic space and feel the pulse of the city's vibrant music scene. With ticket prices typically ranging from €10 to €30, Le Rocher de Palmer offers affordable access to unforgettable live performances. What sets this venue apart is its commitment to showcasing emerging artists alongside established acts, ensuring a rich tapestry of musical experiences for every visitor.

La Cité du Vin: Wine, Music, and Cultural Harmony

In Bordeaux, where wine flows like poetry, La Cité du Vin stands as a testament to the city's rich cultural heritage. While primarily known as a museum dedicated to the art of winemaking, La Cité du Vin also hosts an array of musical events that celebrate the intersection of wine, music, and art. Imagine savoring a glass of fine Bordeaux wine as you listen to the strains of classical music or jazz drifting through the air. Ticket prices for concerts at La Cité du Vin vary depending on the event but typically range from €20 to €50. For a truly immersive experience, consider attending one of their themed musical evenings, where wine tastings complement the melodic journey.

Théâtre Fémina: A Timeless Elegance

Steeped in history and elegance, Théâtre Fémina exudes a timeless charm that beckons music lovers from near and far. Located in the heart of Bordeaux's city center, this majestic concert hall has been a cultural landmark since its opening in 1921. Step through its ornate doors and be transported to a world of refined musical performances, spanning classical recitals, orchestral concerts, and contemporary productions.

Ticket prices at Théâtre Fémina typically range from €20 to €60, depending on the event and seating selection. What sets this venue apart is its impeccable acoustics and intimate atmosphere, ensuring an unforgettable auditory experience for every patron.

Rock School Barbey: Where Amplified Energy Reigns

For those craving the raw energy of live rock and roll, look no further than Rock School Barbey. Tucked away in Bordeaux's Sainte-Croix district, this legendary venue has been a haven for alternative music enthusiasts since the 1980s. From punk and metal to indie and alternative rock, Rock School Barbey hosts an electrifying lineup of concerts that pulse with youthful exuberance. Ticket prices typically range from €15 to €40, making it an accessible destination for music lovers of all ages. What sets this venue apart is its gritty authenticity and unwavering commitment to fostering underground music scenes, ensuring a visceral and unforgettable experience for all who enter its hallowed halls.

Opéra National de Bordeaux: A Symphony of Splendor

Finally, no musical journey through Bordeaux would be complete without a visit to the Opéra National de Bordeaux. Situated in the breathtaking Grand Théâtre de Bordeaux, this prestigious institution is renowned for its world-class opera productions, ballet performances, and classical concerts. Step into its opulent surroundings and marvel at the grandeur of its gilded auditorium, adorned with chandeliers and frescoes that evoke a sense of bygone splendor. Ticket prices at the Opéra National de Bordeaux can vary widely depending on the production and seating selection, but they typically range from €30 to €150. What sets this venue apart is its unwavering dedication to artistic excellence, ensuring an immersive and transcendent musical experience that lingers long after the final curtain falls.

In Bordeaux, music isn't just a form of entertainment—it's a way of life, a symphony of the soul that binds together past and present, tradition and innovation. Whether you're sipping wine at La Cité du Vin, rocking out at Rock School Barbey, or reveling in the grandeur of the Opéra National de Bordeaux, each venue offers a unique glimpse into the city's musical tapestry. So come, let the melody of Bordeaux enchant you, for in its harmonious embrace, you'll discover a world of endless wonder and inspiration.

11.2 Nightclubs and DJ Sets

As a seasoned traveler and author who believes in experiencing destinations firsthand, I've danced my way through countless cities around the world. Yet, there's something truly magical about the nightlife in Bordeaux that keeps drawing me back. In this guide, I invite you to join me on a nocturnal adventure through five of Bordeaux's hottest nightclubs and DJ sets, where the music pulses with the heartbeat of the city, and the dancefloor becomes a canvas for unforgettable memories.

Le Caillou du Jardin Botanique: A Garden of Grooves

Nestled within the enchanting confines of Bordeaux's botanical garden, Le Caillou du Jardin Botanique is a hidden gem for nocturnal revelers. Picture yourself swaying to the rhythm of eclectic beats under a canopy of stars, surrounded by lush greenery and twinkling lights. With its unique outdoor setting and diverse lineup of DJs spinning everything from house and techno to funk and soul, Le Caillou offers a one-of-a-kind nightlife experience. Entry prices typically range from €5 to €15, making it an accessible option for those seeking to dance the night away in a picturesque setting.

I.Boat: Where Music Sets Sail

Perched on the Garonne River, I.Boat is more than just a nightclub—it's a floating haven for music enthusiasts seeking adventure on the dancefloor. Step aboard this converted ferry and prepare to be swept away by its vibrant atmosphere and panoramic views of Bordeaux's waterfront. With multiple stages hosting live bands, DJs, and themed parties, I.Boat promises a diverse musical journey that spans genres and generations. Ticket prices vary depending on the event but typically range from €10 to €20, offering excellent value for an unforgettable night out. What sets I.Boat apart is its ever-evolving lineup of events, ensuring that no two visits are ever the same.

Le Bootleg: Bordeaux's Underground Playground

For those who prefer their nightlife with a side of grit and authenticity, Le Bootleg beckons with its unapologetically underground vibe. Tucked away in the heart of Bordeaux's historic district, this intimate venue pulses with energy as local DJs spin cutting-edge tracks that defy genre boundaries. Step inside its dimly lit interior and lose yourself in the pulsating rhythms and infectious energy of the crowd. Entry prices at Le Bootleg typically range from €5 to €10, making it an affordable option for experiencing Bordeaux's alternative music scene. What sets this venue apart is its commitment to fostering a sense of community among its patrons, creating a space where creativity flourishes and new friendships are forged.

Le Block: Where the Beat Never Stops

Situated in the bustling Saint-Michel neighborhood, Le Block is a temple of electronic music where the beat never stops and the party never ends. With its state-of-the-art sound system and immersive lighting design, this nightclub offers an unparalleled sensory experience for dance music aficionados. Whether you're grooving to the latest techno tracks or losing yourself in a haze of deep house vibes, Le Block promises an electrifying night on the dancefloor. Entry prices typically range from €10 to €20, with occasional special events commanding higher ticket prices. What sets Le Block apart is its dedication to showcasing both local talent and international DJs, ensuring a diverse lineup that keeps the dancefloor pulsating until the early hours of the morning.

La Tencha: A Cultural Hub of Nightlife

At the intersection of music, art, and community, you'll find La Tencha—a cultural hub that transcends the traditional nightclub experience. Located in Bordeaux's vibrant Saint-Pierre district, La Tencha is more than just a place to dance—it's a melting pot of creativity and expression. From live music performances and DJ sets to art exhibitions and spoken word nights, La Tencha offers something for every artistic soul. Entry prices typically range from €5 to €15, depending on the event and time of entry. What sets this venue apart is its inclusive atmosphere and commitment to supporting emerging artists and musicians, making it a must-visit destination for anyone seeking to immerse themselves in Bordeaux's thriving creative scene.

In Bordeaux, the night comes alive with the promise of adventure, discovery, and endless possibilities. Whether you find yourself dancing under the stars at Le Caillou du Jardin Botanique or losing yourself in the hypnotic beats of Le Block, each nightclub and DJ set offers a unique glimpse into the city's vibrant nightlife scene. So come, join me on the dancefloor, and let the rhythm of Bordeaux sweep you away on a journey you'll never forget.

11.3 Cultural Events After Dark

As a seasoned explorer and author who cherishes the richness of firsthand experiences, I've delved deep into the nocturnal soul of Bordeaux, uncovering a treasure trove of cultural events that come alive after dark. In this narrative, I extend an invitation to journey with me through five enchanting cultural soirées, each promising to ignite the imagination and leave an indelible mark on the hearts of those who dare to venture into Bordeaux's after-hours cultural landscape.

The Grand Théâtre de Bordeaux: A Symphony of the Senses

Nestled majestically in the heart of Bordeaux, The Grand Théâtre de Bordeaux stands as a beacon of cultural splendor, drawing aficionados from near and far to its hallowed halls. As twilight descends upon the city, the theater's opulent façade becomes a stage for elegance and refinement, setting the scene for an evening of artistic immersion. Inside, patrons are transported into a world of classical music concerts, ballet performances, and opera productions, each exquisitely crafted to captivate the senses and stir the soul. Ticket prices vary depending on the event and seating selection, but the experience of witnessing a performance within the grandeur of The Grand Théâtre is truly priceless.

The CAPC Museum of Contemporary Art: Where Creativity Shines After Hours

Amidst Bordeaux's historic architecture lies a modern marvel of artistic expression—the CAPC Museum of Contemporary Art. After nightfall, this cultural institution transforms into a haven for the avant-garde, hosting a myriad of after-hours events that push the boundaries of creativity and challenge conventional norms. From late-night gallery openings and multimedia installations to live performances and artist talks, the CAPC Museum offers a dynamic platform for engaging with contemporary art in all its forms. Entry prices typically range from €5 to €10, granting access to a world where imagination knows no limits and innovation reigns supreme.

Darwin: A Hub of Urban Culture Under the Stars

Nestled within the historic confines of a former military barracks, Darwin emerges as a vibrant hub of urban culture that thrives long after the sun sets. As twilight descends upon Bordeaux's riverside, this eclectic space comes alive with a kaleidoscope of cultural events that celebrate creativity, sustainability, and community. Picture yourself meandering through artisanal markets illuminated by twinkling fairy lights, savoring gourmet street food from local vendors, and immersing yourself in live music performances that echo through the night air. Entry to Darwin's events is often free or priced affordably, reflecting its commitment to inclusivity and accessibility for all who seek to partake in its cultural offerings.

Les Vivres de l'Art: Where Art Flourishes After Dark

In the heart of Bordeaux's Chartrons district, Les Vivres de l'Art emerges as a beacon of artistic innovation that ignites the imagination long after the city's streets have emptied. As dusk descends, this former military compound becomes a canvas for creative expression, hosting a myriad of nighttime events that blur the lines between art, music, and performance. From immersive multimedia installations and experimental theater productions to interactive workshops and underground concerts, Les Vivres de l'Art offers a sensory journey into the heart of Bordeaux's avant-garde scene. Entry prices vary depending on the event but are often modest, ensuring that cultural enrichment remains accessible to all who seek it.

La Nuit des Musées: A Night of Cultural Exploration

Once a year, Bordeaux's cultural institutions open their doors after hours for a special event known as La Nuit des Musées, inviting visitors to embark on a nocturnal journey of discovery and delight. From the majestic halls of the Musée d'Aquitaine to the intimate galleries of the Musée des Beaux-Arts, museums across the city come alive with a wealth of activities, including guided tours, live performances, and interactive exhibits. Entry to La Nuit des Musées is typically free of charge, offering a rare opportunity for locals and visitors alike to immerse themselves in the rich tapestry of Bordeaux's cultural heritage under the cover of night.

In Bordeaux, the setting sun heralds not the end of exploration, but the beginning of a new chapter in the city's cultural narrative. From the grandeur of The Grand Théâtre to the avant-garde allure of Darwin, each after-dark cultural event promises to ignite the senses, provoke thought, and inspire wonder. So come, dear reader, and immerse yourself in the nocturnal wonders of Bordeaux, where the night is alive with the promise of discovery and delight.

11.4 Late-Night Eats and Hangouts

As a veteran traveler and connoisseur of culinary delights, I've learned that a city's true essence often reveals itself after the sun sets. In Bordeaux, where gastronomic wonders abound, the late-night hours offer a tantalizing array of eateries and hangouts where locals and visitors alike gather to indulge in the pleasures of the palate. Join me as we embark on a nocturnal journey through five of Bordeaux's most enticing late-night eats and hangouts, where the flavors are as vibrant as the city itself.

La Tupina: A Taste of Tradition

Nestled in the heart of Bordeaux's historic Saint-Pierre district, La Tupina beckons with the promise of rustic charm and culinary authenticity. As the night deepens, this beloved eatery transforms into a haven for gastronomes seeking traditional French fare served with a side of conviviality. Picture yourself seated at a weathered wooden table, surrounded by the warm glow of candlelight, as you savor hearty dishes such as confit de canard and grilled entrecôte. While prices at La Tupina may lean towards the higher end, ranging from €30 to €50 per person for a meal, the experience of dining in this legendary establishment is worth every penny. What sets La Tupina apart is its commitment to preserving Bordeaux's culinary heritage, making it a must-visit destination for anyone seeking an authentic taste of the region.

L'Autre Petit Bois: Where Tapas Reign Supreme

For those craving a taste of Spain in the heart of Bordeaux, look no further than L'Autre Petit Bois. Tucked away on a quaint side street near Place Fernand Lafargue, this intimate tapas bar exudes a lively ambiance that draws in locals and visitors alike. As the night unfolds, patrons gather around wooden tables adorned with plates of tantalizing small bites, from patatas bravas to gambas al ajillo. With prices typically ranging from €5 to €10 per dish, L'Autre Petit Bois offers a wallet-friendly option for late-night indulgence. What sets this tapas bar apart is its eclectic selection of dishes, each bursting with bold flavors and made from the freshest local ingredients.

Le Comptoir du Jazz: A Melodic Feast for the Senses

Nestled along the picturesque Quai de Paludate, Le Comptoir du Jazz offers a symphony of flavors and melodies that enchant the senses long into the night. As the sounds of live jazz spill out onto the cobblestone streets, patrons gather inside this cozy bistro to savor a menu inspired by the rhythms of New Orleans. From succulent barbecue ribs to creamy étouffée, each dish is a culinary masterpiece that pays homage to the vibrant culture of jazz. While prices at Le Comptoir du Jazz may vary depending on the dish and time of visit, patrons can expect to pay between €15 and €30 for a satisfying meal. What sets this bistro apart is its intimate atmosphere and live music performances, creating a dining experience that is as soulful as it is delicious.

Chez Jean-Mi: A Gastronomic Oasis in the Night*

In the heart of Bordeaux's Chartrons district, Chez Jean-Mi emerges as a beacon of culinary excellence that shines brightest after dark. Tucked away on a charming side street, this cozy bistro offers a menu of seasonal delights that celebrate the bounty of the region. Picture yourself seated at a candlelit table, savoring dishes such as foie gras terrine and truffle risotto, expertly paired with wines from Bordeaux's renowned vineyards. While prices at Chez Jean-Mi may lean towards the higher end, ranging from €40 to €60 per person for a meal, the experience of dining in this gastronomic oasis is nothing short of unforgettable. What sets Chez Jean-Mi apart is its commitment to using locally sourced ingredients and innovative cooking techniques, ensuring a culinary journey that delights the palate and nourishes the soul.

La Cité du Vin: A Toast to the Night

Perched on the banks of the Garonne River, La Cité du Vin invites travelers to embark on a nocturnal voyage of discovery and indulgence. As the lights of Bordeaux shimmer in the distance, patrons gather inside this iconic wine museum to savor an array of gourmet delights paired with the finest vintages from around the world. From wine tastings and culinary workshops to themed dinners and soirées, La Cité du Vin offers a wealth of experiences that celebrate the art of wine and gastronomy.

While prices for events at La Cité du Vin may vary depending on the experience, patrons can expect to pay between €20 and €100 for an unforgettable evening of culinary exploration. What sets this venue apart is its stunning architecture and panoramic views of the city, creating a backdrop that is as breathtaking as the wines it showcases.

In Bordeaux, the night is not just a time for rest—it's a canvas for culinary exploration and gastronomic delight. Whether you find yourself savoring traditional French fare at La Tupina or tapping your toes to the rhythm of live jazz at Le Comptoir du Jazz, each late-night eatery and hangout promises to ignite the senses and leave a lasting impression. So come, dear reader, and indulge in the nocturnal wonders of Bordeaux, where every bite and sip is a symphony of flavor and a toast to the joys of the night.

CONCLUSION AND INSIDER TIPS

As we draw the curtains on our journey through Bordeaux, I can't help but feel a sense of awe at the tapestry of experiences this city has to offer. From its historic landmarks and cultural institutions to its vibrant culinary scene and dynamic nightlife, Bordeaux is a destination that captures the imagination and leaves an indelible mark on the soul of every traveler. As a veteran explorer and author who believes in the power of firsthand experience, I've had the privilege of immersing myself in Bordeaux's rich tapestry of sights, sounds, and flavors. And now, as I bid farewell to this enchanting city, I leave you with a few insider tips to ensure that your own journey to Bordeaux is nothing short of extraordinary.

Insider Tips for Visitors: Unlocking the Secrets of Bordeaux

Embrace the Art of Slow Travel: In a city as rich in history and culture as Bordeaux, it's essential to slow down and savor each moment. Take the time to wander through its charming streets, linger in its picturesque squares, and soak up the ambiance of its bustling markets. The true essence of Bordeaux reveals itself to those who are willing to pause and appreciate the beauty that surrounds them.

Explore Beyond the Guidebooks: While Bordeaux's iconic landmarks are certainly worth a visit, don't be afraid to stray off the beaten path and explore its hidden gems. Venture into the city's lesser-known neighborhoods, where you'll discover quaint cafes, artisan boutiques, and local markets brimming with fresh produce and handmade treasures. It's in these hidden corners that you'll find the true heart and soul of Bordeaux.

Indulge in the Culinary Delights: Bordeaux is a food lover's paradise, with an abundance of restaurants, bistros, and cafes serving up delectable dishes inspired by the region's rich culinary heritage. Don't miss the opportunity to sample Bordeaux's world-renowned wines, paired with local specialties such as foie gras, oysters, and hearty cassoulet. And be sure to save room for dessert—Bordeaux's pastries and sweets are not to be missed.

Immerse Yourself in the Arts: From its stunning architecture to its vibrant arts scene, Bordeaux is a city that inspires creativity and expression. Take in a performance at The Grand Théâtre de Bordeaux, explore the contemporary art galleries of the CAPC Museum, or simply stroll through the city streets, where every corner seems to tell a story. Whether you're a lover of fine art or simply appreciate beauty in all its forms, Bordeaux offers a wealth of cultural experiences to delight and inspire.

Embrace the Joie de Vivre: Above all else, remember to embrace the joie de vivre—the joy of life—that permeates every aspect of Bordeaux. Whether you're sipping wine by the river, dancing the night away in a local nightclub, or simply basking in the warmth of the sun in one of Bordeaux's many parks, take the time to revel in the simple pleasures that make life worth living. In Bordeaux, every moment is an opportunity to create memories that will last a lifetime.

As you turn the pages of this travel guide and prepare to embark on your own adventure to Bordeaux, I hope you carry with you a sense of excitement and anticipation for the experiences that lie ahead. Whether you're a first-time visitor or a seasoned traveler returning to this beloved city, may your journey be filled with wonder, discovery, and moments of pure joy. Bordeaux awaits, dear reader—let its magic sweep you away on a journey you'll never forget.

Printed in Great Britain
by Amazon